D1495342

020
X20
1000

The
Pianist's
Problems

Other Books by William S. Newman

UNDERSTANDING MUSIC

A HISTORY OF THE SONATA IDEA:

THE SONATA IN THE BAROQUE ERA

THE SONATA IN THE CLASSIC ERA

THE SONATA SINCE BEETHOVEN

PERFORMANCE PRACTICES IN BEETHOVEN'S
PIANO SONATAS: AN INTRODUCTION

The
PIANIST'S
PROBLEMS

A MODERN APPROACH
TO EFFICIENT PRACTICE AND
MUSICIANLY PERFORMANCE

THIRD EXPANDED EDITION

William S. Newman

The University of North Carolina at Chapel Hill

With a Preface by Arthur Loesser
Illustrated by John V. Allcott

HARPER & ROW, PUBLISHERS
New York, Evanston, San Francisco, London

THE PIANIST'S PROBLEMS: A MODERN APPROACH TO EFFICIENT PRACTICE AND
MUSICIANLY PERFORMANCE, THIRD EXPANDED EDITION. Copyright © 1950, 1956
by Harper & Row, Publishers, Inc. Copyright © 1974 by William S. Newman.
All rights reserved. Printed in the United States of America. No part of this book
may be used or reproduced in any manner whatsoever without written permission
except in the case of brief quotations embodied in critical articles and reviews.
For information address Harper & Row, Publishers, Inc., 10 East 53rd Street,
New York, N.Y. 10022. Published simultaneously in Canada by Fitzhenry &
Whiteside Limited, Toronto.

Library of Congress Cataloging in Publication Data

Newman, William S
  The pianist's problems.
  Bibliography: p. 200
  1. Piano—Practicing. I. Title.
MT220.N5 1974   786.3'04'1   73-14275
ISBN 0-06-013181-0

To my students,
who, by being students,
have compelled me to crystallize
these thoughts on
piano playing

Contents

Foreword
by Arthur Loesser

THE PIANIST has his problems. It is by solving them that he enters upon the delights of piano playing. Why must these problems be? For answer, we must acknowledge that some of them are inherent in the paradoxical nature of the piano itself.

To begin with, the piano appears as one of the most mechanical of all instruments. Fiddlers and pipers are appalled at the levers upon levers that interpose between the source of the piano tone and the player's bodily impulse. Yet this mechanical complexity is no end in itself. Nor is it designed as a means to any sort of automatism. Its real purpose is to provide a tool that will respond with maximum sensitivity to the human touch. Each lever, each regulator that has been added over the years has enabled the tones to reflect just so much more faithfully the variety of impacts that the hands can produce.

But because of this mechanical complexity, piano playing is always in danger of falling into a dry, prosaic clatter. The player is allowed only the one tiny instant while the hammer is in contact with the string to produce the desired live tone. However, for the clever player that instant is enough. On a good piano the resonance of the tone—its remains, its corpse, if you will—may have a beauty of its own, which he can mold to an exquisite, artistic purpose. To be sure, the pianist must be a sophisticated, canny fellow if he wishes to count as a musician in this way. He will need more than the simpler instincts that guide the singer, for he must know how to cajole, almost to cheat, the music out of the great ironbound structure of the piano.

The piano poses other paradoxes. Unlike the violin, the difficulties of which are apparent from the start, the piano is deceptively easy to play acceptably in the early stages of learning. But to achieve its higher capabilities becomes difficult out of all proportion. Little time goes by before the aspiring pianist runs up against problems of muscular coordination, of mental grasp that fewer and fewer can surmount.

Then, too, we think of the piano as the universal instrument for performers and composers alike. How impressive is the array of saints and heroes of musical creation who have entrusted some of their most valuable thoughts to it! Yet, there have been musicians, some of them great composers, whose affections have been inaccessible to the peculiar genius of the piano. Thus, the piano remains the most practical, the most complete among instruments, yet the most refractory—ready to frustrate its bunglers but to reward its craftier, more diligent devotees with a matchless exhilaration.

Fortunately, the prognosis for the pianist's problems is good. Eighty years ago a writer called the piano "the leading musical instrument of Christendom." If it has since declined somewhat from that pre-eminence, the decline may be regarded as extensive rather than intensive. No longer is piano playing generally degraded into a shallow, showy "accomplishment" for genteel young ladies. It is studied by fewer persons today, perhaps, than formerly, but it is studied with much more intelligence and honesty of purpose.

The newer attitude toward piano study has made obsolete some of the older ideas. Inevitably, modern practitioners view its problems from modern perspectives and quite properly pass on to others the benefits of their enlightenment. William Newman is a skillful pianist. What is more, he is a man of thought, enterprise, and experience. He has overcome many a difficulty of his own. He has understood and helped to lighten the difficulties of many others. We do well to hear him with interest and respect.

Cleveland, Ohio, May 1949

Preface to the First Edition (1950)

THE IMMEDIATE IMPETUS for this book came from a recent lecture-recital tour of colleges and universities in the Midwest, during which I was much impressed by an eager interest in everything that was practical and up-to-date about piano playing. The intention to write the book goes further back, however. For some time I had been promising students and teachers in my department that I would put down in writing a straightforward account of what I felt "every pianist ought to know." My thought was to supply those essential principles of practice, technique, and musicianly playing that can best be had from a book, leaving the lesson time freer for intangible problems that are better illustrated and tried over "in person."

The actual writing has proved to be one of the most satisfying tasks that I can recall undertaking, no doubt because it relates throughout to experiences that I myself have lived and believed. There is a satisfaction, too, in getting down to earth—in probing problems of everyday concern to student and teacher. Perhaps the very ordinariness of these problems has kept a good many of them from being considered in other books on piano playing. Or perhaps other factors are responsible. In any case, I would hardly be the first to cite their neglect as a characteristic failing among all too many books of this sort. Glib generalizations abound that cannot be translated into practicalities. "The secret of my method" is heralded in prefaces, yet never gets divulged because such a secret does not exist outside the aura of the writer's personality.

The main point, I suppose, is that the great artists are rightly too preoccupied with their art to investigate what must seem to them to be mundane details of learning. It is a truism to state that successful performers do not necessarily make knowing teachers. Repeatedly, the acknowledged artist, seeking to account for something that his talents enable him to do without effort, attempts to guide others with explanations and procedures that directly contradict basic tenets of the physiologist, the psychologist, and, yes, even the composer.

This charge leads me to what is at least a pretty rationalization and at most a valid justification for this book. I like to see an analogy in Oliver Wendell Holmes's country doctor, who was all the better in his profession for having been a sickly man himself. A Rubinstein or a Horowitz might wonder what the obstacle was, where a lesser man could advise, "Try this; I found it to help when I experienced the same difficulty."

The Pianist's Problems (originally called by the bulkier if catchier title *Are You Wasting Time at the Piano?*) was allowed to "simmer" for several months before publication was undertaken. During those months more students, teachers, and other colleagues from all parts of the country read and commented on the original manuscript than I can possibly list here to thank. They will know how indebted I am to them when they see their extremely useful suggestions incorporated here. However, I do mean to single out the eminent American composer and pianist Arthur Shepherd, and that peerless performer and teacher Arthur Loesser, who have commented so choicely that I have decided to insert their reactions as verbatim quotations where they apply rather than to lose these in the text.

And Now a
Third Edition (1974)

THIS THIRD TIME AROUND, eighteen years have passed since the latest edition of a book that was originally written twenty-five years ago. If the basic philosophies regarding musicianship, technique, interpretation, and performance still hold firm in *The Pianist's Problems,* there has been much more occasion this time to make changes and additions. In fact, a page-by-page comparison would show not merely that the book has been completely reset but that Chapters 2 through 4 have been reorganized and expanded into the present Chapters 2 through 5, that the whole book has been enlarged by about a fourth, that the number of music examples has been nearly doubled (to forty-five), and that everything has been updated—especially lists, tables, and references, as well as certain of the original ideas—wherever updating has seemed desirable. (The updating has stopped short, however, of "prepared" piano, stroking of the strings themselves, and other new uses of the instrument. Significant as these uses may or may not prove to be in today's composing, they break so radically with all past uses that they still find no place in the mainstream of "the pianist's problems.")

Some of the added material is new. Some represents the greater penetration of subject matter that I have been encouraged to make by a general rise in the sophistication and caliber of teaching and student performance around the country over the last quarter century. And some grows out of an effort to achieve still greater clarity and precision in each explanation, with still fuller illustrations, to the point where scarcely a paragraph has survived without at least some detail being altered.

Among portions not changed or deleted are the intermittent comments by Arthur Loesser and Arthur Shepherd. These comments, which originated as reactions to the first draft of this book, remain as valid, applicable, and fresh as ever, even though their distinguished authors are no longer with us to supply the living proof. Further valued comments have come from other esteemed musicians in many parts of this country and in numerous foreign countries right up to the time of the present revision. I have tried to acknowledge these individually as they have come in and would like to express further thanks here. Of particular interest have been the extended comments and correspondence received from the eminent pianists and teachers Wiktor Labunski of Kansas City, Missouri, and John Dielhenn of Princeton, New Jersey. I hope they will detect my appreciation in the way some of these comments have been woven into the changes and additions.

And finally, I owe my wife special thanks for her continued indispensable help in spite of my continued violation of solemn promises to quit writing and rewriting books.

W.S.N.

The
Pianist's
Problems

. . . the ordering of exercises is matter of great consequence to hurt or help; for, as is well observed by Cicero, men in exercising their faculties, if they be not well advised, do exercise their faults and get ill habits as well as good; so there is great judgment to be had in the continuance and intermission of exercises.

Francis Bacon, *The Advancement of Learning*

A Preview of the Problems

THE READER MUST have noted in the *Piano Quarterly, Clavier,* and other favorite magazines of the practicing pianist how often the same troubled queries reappear: How can memorizing be made easier and more secure? Which exercises yield the best results?

What is to be done about stage fright? Why are some editions better than others? How can the fourth and fifth fingers be strengthened? What produces musicianship? These and many others are perennial questions of the greatest practical importance to student, teacher, and performer. Strange,, then, that adequate answers are so hard to find. With all the time and effort devoted to the study of the piano, with all the advances in the psychology of training, with all the special studies that have been conducted, there should be, by now, if not one right answer to each question, at least a preferred answer that will be right for the large majority of pianists.

As a matter of fact, there are preferred answers in almost every instance. They alone hardly account for what makes great pianists great; but they can afford substantial help to those of us with average talents who hope to avoid the pitfalls and smooth out the tortuous road from beginner to accomplished pianist. Such answers have grown out of the specific research of scholars like Breithaupt and Ortmann, out of the inspired doctrines of teachers like Leschetizky, Matthay, and Busoni, and out of the wide experience of countless students who have had to learn their methods the hard way. The need is to bring these answers together, in one place, and to present them in nontechnical language as a concise, up-to-date, coordinated philosophy of piano playing. To meet this need, the present book has been written.

The first five chapters are organized according to the four main problems of any applied music study—Musicianship, Technique, Practice, and Performance. Then follows a chapter illustrating more specifically how these problems may be met in the successive stages of learning. The final chapter considers two highly pertinent questions of teaching method. Of course, a full discussion of piano problems would fill many volumes. Therefore, the emphasis here must be on things that give the most trouble and those that seem to be most basic, or neglected, or controversial. The ideas presented here have been borne out by my own day-by-day experience as performer, teacher, and student, a fact that will perhaps excuse the several references to myself. Some of these ideas represent complete reversals of ideas formerly handed down to me. Many of them will not be found in other books. However, I can hardly claim that the large number of them are either original with me or unique. They also represent, in frequent instances, the experience of my pianist

friends in diverse schools throughout the country and the conclusions reached in various scientific and controlled studies.

To whom, then, is this book primarily addressed? To the student
and teacher alike who are eager to make the most of their respec-
tive talents; to each in turn, since each must understand the other's
problems as well as his own in order to get the fullest view. There
are others, too, for whom I hope the book will be of value. Artist
performers may be able to pick up a useful pointer here and there;
interested parents may gain an insight into the pianist in the making; and piano pedagogy classes may find not only some new blood
in the book's ideas but also a practical sequence of these ideas such
as is necessary in a class text.

One other point should be made now. Except for the beginning
year or so (as discussed in the final chapter), what is said here
applies in principle and within the limits of comprehension as
much to pianists at one age or level as another. Differences in the
problems of young and adult students are commonly exaggerated.
We tend to underestimate both the intellectual and interpretative
powers of the child, on the one hand, and the ability of the adult
to learn new skills, on the other. Yet it is remarkable how early
and quickly a child can learn to count or transpose, how soon he
takes pleasure in the simplest music of Bach and Chopin. As for
the adult, his problem lies not, as he supposes, in relative speed
of advancement—for he usually learns at least as rapidly as the
child—but in his attitude toward his progress. Too often he is
impatient because his more mature tastes and interests remain far
ahead of his abilities and because he takes too analytical and self-
conscious a view of his learning behavior.

Perfectly sound learning may seem very erratic when examined
step by step. The student may fail to realize, for example, that the
ascent into the higher regions of his skill will not be a steady one.
Instead, he must pause time and time again as he reaches temporary
limits to the amount of material that he can grasp. At each of
these limits he will find himself on a plateau where he seems to

bog down for a while. Actually, the plateau marks the period during which he assimilates what he has just struggled to learn. Then, no sooner is the assimilation complete than he must ascend to another level of new material. This new ascent may discourage him, too, because it tends to upset the security he has just achieved. Yet, such is the bumpy, stepwise path along which true learning progresses.

1. Musicianship

THE ASPECTS of musicianship discussed here involve skills and experiences outside the assigned lesson yet fundamental to artistic judgment and technical mastery in performance. Of far-reaching significance to the pianist are the abilities to play by ear, to read at sight, and to participate in ensembles. Much too often these abilities fail to be cultivated at the lesson because their importance to learning and performance is not understood, because they are left to general theory and musicianship classes where the special problems of piano playing can hardly receive adequate attention, because the more immediate goals of solo performance pre-empt all of the lesson time, or simply because the teacher himself is deficient in them. Yet the growing number of successful beginners' books that include musicianship drills and the increasing place that musicianship courses are taking in applied music curricula are encouraging evidence that the need for such abilities is gaining wider recognition, from the student's very first lesson to his most advanced coaching.

Actually, it was the fashion some years ago to discourage playing at sight or by ear as a distraction, even a harmful influence, in the regular assigned lesson. To be sure, these practices are pleasurable to a degree that may tempt the student away from slower, more exacting tasks; and in their very informality they do tend to encourage slovenliness, at least in those who fail to develop habits of neatness and precision anyway. But, like the newest and best medical drugs, when wisely administered in proper doses they may work wonders. It is well to have the student save his playing by ear and at sight for, say, the last ten per cent of his practice time, when he will be ready for his dessert, so to speak—that is, for the diversion that these skills offer, without any danger of cutting deeply into the time for his assigned pieces. Ensemble playing should get at least one session a week. After these skills have been introduced and explained, the teacher need give only a fraction of the lesson to them, ordinarily just enough to make certain they are being followed up correctly.

But a more satisfactory opportunity to develop these important peripheral skills is the class musicianship session that more and more progressive teachers are adding to the private lesson each week. Scheduling groups of up to eight of their students with similar backgrounds, such teachers find they can teach more efficiently not only playing by ear, at sight, and in ensembles but also numerous other skills ranging from staff reading and rhythm clapping to form analysis and style discrimination by eras. Learning together makes the difference. One should never forget that music has always thrived mainly in society. The violinist in an orchestra or clarinetist in a band enjoys social incentives lacking to those piano students who are expected to do all their learning in isolation.

On Learning to Play by Ear

The values of being able to play by ear are several. In the first place, there is a marked correlation between this ability and the ability to memorize. Of course, as will be seen, other factors enter equally into memorizing. Yet, almost invariably, the student who cannot play by ear memorizes slowly or insecurely. Second, for reasons to be discussed presently, there is a marked correlation between the ability to play by ear and the ability to sight-read. Third, playing by ear contributes to that elusive quality of good

piano playing, fluency. It does this both by developing a harmonic grasp that perceives notes in intelligible groups rather than one at a time and by providing a new wealth of practical experiences. Finally, by translating to the piano a mental concept recorded by ear, rather than a printed page recorded by eye, the student does much to heighten his harmonic, melodic, and rhythmic acuity.

What should be played by ear? Anything and everything that appeals and that can be culled from the memory. This is most likely to include folk-type music, familiar themes from standard classics, and jazz. It is less likely to include contrapuntal or extreme modern music, although the student does no harm in trying to recall these. Improvising, too, has certain values, but it requires special discipline if it is not to fall into stereotyped idioms and progressions that lead nowhere. Do not disavow jazz, which figures in any balanced diet and, needless to say, is one important part of our American culture. Time after time the contention that jazz players cannot adapt themselves to serious concert music is disproved.

Occasionally we meet a student who retains tunes very poorly, perhaps remembering nothing at all in its entirety. It may be that he has never done anything to exercise his musical memory, such as singing in community groups or during the day's activities at home. Even so, he is still evincing one kind of musical shortcoming that may or may not be counterbalanced by strengths in other musical attributes. One help for such a student is to provide him with a book of folk and familiar melodies. He can then sing and memorize one of these at a time, the ultimate goal being to supply his own accompaniments. The student's frequent plea that he is a monotone generally should be discredited. An actual monotone is about as rare as an actual case of ptomaine poisoning.

Teachers discover that new students vary widely in their ability to play by ear. Some have trained themselves surprisingly well, merely needing guidance in creating more interesting accompaniments and in choosing more purposeful or varied harmony. Others have to struggle even to pick out a one-finger melody. Only too often a student will be playing advanced works without any sense of an aural approach to the piano. In this person's playing, the deficiency will crop up in many subtle and unexpected ways, often resulting in a halting, unmusical performance.

At this point, Mr. Arthur Loesser, who kindly provided extremely conscientious and helpful reactions to an earlier draft of this book, remarked:

> Check and double check to everything you say about playing by ear. But what will you do with the earnest soul who cannot even get started at it? There are ever so many students, alas, to whom the keyboard is a completely lifeless mechanism, who cannot mentally associate a key with a tone until after they have struck it. Oh yes, they can learn to play a Chopin etude sometimes, but they cannot find the "Star-Spangled Banner" in E-flat. What medicine for them?

My prescription follows in some detail, since playing by ear seems to be as vague as it is necessary for a good many pianists.

If the student must start in from the beginning to learn to play by ear, then he must have some preparatory work. Because the skill must be not only intuitive but under conscious, intellectual control, at least an elementary knowledge of scales, keys, intervals, and chords—in short, of the musician's everyday jargon—is prerequisite. It may be introduced about as outlined here. (Elsewhere I have provided a more general introduction to music theory, styles, and forms, as noted in the listing for *Understanding Music* among Source References on page 203).

How to build major scales may be taught in two easy stages:

1. Learn the meaning of whole- and half-steps. Distinguish them by ear; sing them; play them. Always name them as adjacent letters.
2. Build a scale on each of the twelve chromatic tones according to the whole- and half-step pattern 1–1–½ 1–1–1–½. Do this (*a*) on paper, (*b*) reciting the successive letter names at the piano, and (*c*) singing them away from the piano. In spelling the tones, never repeat or skip a letter and never mix flats with sharps, even though these rules sometimes necessitate the use of double-sharps or double-flats.

Key relationships may readily be taught by the familiar circle (or clock) of fifths, with emphasis on the "magic number" five:

1. Draw a circle and enter C, representing the key of no accidentals, where noon shows on the clock. Then, counting up a *perfect* fifth each time, enter the sharp keys in the order of 1 to 7 sharps where the corresponding hours would fall on the clock.
2. Similarly, enter the seven flat keys counterclockwise where the numbers 11 to 5 would fall, by counting perfect fifths *down* from C. Note especially that there are six overlapping or *enharmonic* keys (at 5, 6, and 7 on the clock), thus leaving only twelve actual out of fifteen theoretical keys.
3. Determine the order of the sharps themselves (F–C–G–D–A–E–B) and of the flats (the same sequence reversed), again by counting perfect fifths up and down, respectively.

Intervals are best presented as though the lower note is the tonic of a major scale. Since the other tones of the major scale always form a major or perfect interval with the tonic, the upper note of the interval may easily be compared with the inflection it would have in the major scale. Thus, in the augmented sixth B♭–G♯, the G-sharp may be compared with the G-natural that belongs in the major scale of B-flat.

Finally, traditional chord structure is explained with no difficulty to the student who knows his scales. Triads and sevenths may be erected on the root indicated by the roman numeral or the name for any scale degree simply by selecting every other letter. For instance, in the key of A, the IV or subdominant chord is the chord built on D, the fourth scale degree, and formed in this way: DEF♯GA.

For a concentrated, catchall drill that includes chords, intervals, and minor as well as major keys, the student may invent questions according to the following pattern, preferably answering them away from the piano:

> *Question.* What are the tones and what intervals do they define in the III triad of the harmonic minor scale of five sharps?
>
> *Answer.* B, D-sharp, F-double-sharp; major third and major third, totaling an augmented fifth.

The variables in this question are, of course, the choice of triad (from I to VII), of mode (major or any kind of minor), and of the number (one to seven) and kind (sharp or flat) of accidentals.

Students who are woefully weak in the intuitive side of playing by ear may also need the help of other preliminaries such as these:

1. Sight-sing the letter names and conduct the meter of simple melodies like those found in singing books used in the grammar grades. Do this away from the piano, working out the leaps by thinking through the intervening tones.
2. Do the same with familiar melodies from memory. (See below on how to find the starting tone.)
3. At the piano, transpose hymns and folk-tune arrangements such as those found in community songbooks. Choose both near and distant keys.

4. Play basic, cadential chord progressions like the two in Example 1, which may be continued clockwise and counterclockwise, respectively, around the circle of keys. Always use the same fingerings and chord positions. Shift octaves as necessary so as to remain at the center of the piano.

EXAMPLE 1

These skills may seem far removed from actual piano playing. Yet they have a direct bearing on playing by ear and so contribute in many ways to the rounded musicianship of successful performers.

To extend his feel for the keyboard, the student should choose a new key, moving clockwise around the circle of fifths, each time he plays another piece by ear. To develop his control he should make certain that he can count out the meter of whatever he plays by ear. The prime necessity for counting as a means to authoritative rhythm in performance will be discussed later. Here the important consideration is the interrelation of meter and chord change in the traditional harmony that the student uses to play by ear. The rule of thumb that requires a change of chord or bass over the bar (that is, from "weak" to "strong" beat) may be familiar

enough to him, but he can hardly apply it if he does not know
where the bars occur in his tune. Similarly, the correct use of the
appoggiatura and other nonharmonic tones depends on metric
relationships. Thus, one learns to watch for a tone on the first beat
when it is quitted stepwise, up or down, knowing that it will
usually sound most convincing when treated as an appoggiatura—
that is, as a nonharmonic tone that sideslips into one of the tones
of the next chord rather than a harmonic tone in a chord of its
own. For instance, at the opening of "Annie Laurie" we ordinarily
prefer the second alternative in Example 2.

EXAMPLE 2

This is not the place for any more extended review of keyboard
harmony, but a few suggestions as to procedure may again be
helpful to interested pianists. The usual problem is to recall a tune
and to provide it with a correct, if not *the* correct, harmonic accompaniment. The student does well, first, to pick out the tune alone
and learn to count it. Pausing to figure out the interval in the
"mind's ear" is better than haphazard, hunt-and-peck trial and
error. The initial difficulty of determining what tone of the scale
the tune starts on is usually met by establishing the chosen key
with a simple I–IV–V–I cadence. Then, if the tonic chord is
played with each of its notes on top in turn, the student will
ordinarily hear one of them as the starting tone or a neighbor of
the starting tone (most familiar tunes begin on one of the tones
of the tonic triad). The student will do best at first to play only

the melody in his right hand with an *um-pah-pah* (bass-chord-chord), *um-pah-um-pah*, or *um-pah-pah-pah* accompaniment in the left. The *um* will ordinarily be the chord root played one to three octaves below the right hand. The *pah* will be the chord complete or, which is often better, the chord minus the tone being played in the melody, its position usually centering around middle C or as near to the right hand as is possible without interference.

It is essential for the student to realize that a strong, satisfactory harmony may be found solely with the use of the I, IV, and V chords, since these define the basic directions of all harmonic movement and since they contain every tone of the scale. If he masters just these primary chords, he will have gone a long way toward meeting the pianist's need for playing by ear. A sensible way for him to approach them is to determine first the focal harmonies at the main structural divisions in the tune, then the intermediary chords, just as he might prepare an English theme by first outlining the idea, then filling in the detail. Actually, there is not much choice. The problem is primarily one of learning to sense the "feel" of the proper triad and the moment when a change to a new triad is needed.

In the following diagram, which shows the tonic (I) as a chord of repose between the counterbalanced, suspensive chords of the subdominant (IV) and dominant (V), it is apparent that only the first and fifth scale degrees (C and G) are members of more than one chord.

```
            I
         C  E  G
   F  A  C     G  B  D
     IV           V
```

Each of the other degrees can belong to only one chord (unless it is treated as a chord seventh in descending melodies, which happens most often when the fourth scale degree is accompanied by the dominant harmony). As for the choice of chords on the first and fifth degrees, sometimes one of these will immediately sound much better than the other to the student; at other times either will do, depending only on personal taste. In Example 3, note that there is little question about the chord for the first C and G, no question about that for A, and a choice on the final G, depending on whether a less or more suspensive ending is preferred.

EXAMPLE 3

Generally, as the *rate of harmonic rhythm* (frequency of chord change) decreases, the fluency of an accompaniment, and hence the likely speed of the piece, increases. (To use a remote but helpful analogy, the lighter the food the more readily we can digest it; we can devour angel food cake in huge gulps whereas we must restrict fruitcake to small bites.) As the harmonic rhythm slows, more and more melody notes become *passing* (stepwise) notes between the notes of the adjacent chords (like D and F in Example 3 or the D so indicated in Example 6). Folk and community songs, dances, and marches are characterized by slow harmonic rhythm. By contrast, most hymns and most slow music are characterized by fast harmonic rhythm, in which the chord changes may occur as often as once per melody note, with almost no passing notes. The intuitive ear is the best guide as to where and how often to change the chord.

After the student shows a musicianly command of the fundamental harmonies, which chiefly means sensing the full and half cadences, avoiding parallelisms between IV and V, and choosing the chords that best accommodate the melodic outline, he may attempt other harmonies. To such a student certain additional procedures are recommended. These may be introduced in easy stages as their need arises:

First come the familiar full-cadence formulas, especially ii–V–I and I$^6_4$–V–I or their variants, as at the end of "Old Folks at Home" and of "Battle Hymn of the Republic" in Example 4. These formulas quickly become identified with characteristic melodic closes, the 2–2–1 and 8–7–8 scale progressions in this same example being very common ones.

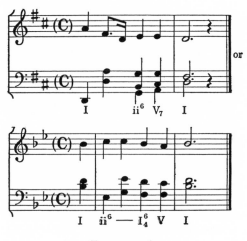

EXAMPLE 4

Second comes the principal dominant embellishment, the major triad or seventh chord erected on II. This secondary dominant (V of V) permits temporary modulations to the dominant key and more varied half cadences, as at the midpoint of Haydn's "Emperor" theme, in Example 5.

Next, the student may try his hand at the use of other dominant embellishments (*applied* dominants), or rather at the use of any of the triads I to vi, preceded by *its own* dominant harmony. In effect, he will be establishing temporary dominant-tonic relationships between weak and strong beats at suitable points in the melody. Although this procedure could soon become overdone

EXAMPLE 5

in simple folk songs, it furnishes a valuable guide to students learning to play by ear. Stated briefly, any melody tone that falls on a strong beat may be harmonized as root, third, fifth, or even seventh (or as an appoggiatura of one of these) of any major or minor chord in the original key *provided* the melody permits the particular dominant of that chord to occur on the preceding weak beat (or beats).

More explicitly, in this last procedure these observations will normally apply:

1. To find the temporary tonics, systematically test each strong-beat tone to determine what major or minor chord within the key it might be the root of, what the third, and so on. Thus, in the key of G, B might be treated as the root of the iii, the third of the I, or the fifth of the vi chord. Any of these may be selected if its own dominant (that is, the major chords on F-sharp, D, and B, respectively, in the examples just cited) does not clash unintelligibly with the foregoing melody.

2. Foreign accidentals (altered tones) will be required for the embellishing dominants (thus, the E-major chord is the dominant of vi in C) but not for the temporary tonics (disregarding the possibility of "borrowed" tones).

3. Strong and weak beats are determined by the barline and the tempo. In slower music, the first beat of a measure will be a strong beat (as will the third beat in four-quarter meter) and the other beats will be weak. In faster music, corresponding relationships occur in the grouping of the measures. Thus, in the

waltz and quick march time, the embellishing dominant will often occupy an entire "weak" measure so that an applied dominant and its temporary tonic may alternate in two-measure groups. Greater harmonic stability and smoothness is achieved, in any case, by placing the embellishing dominant as early in its measure as the melody permits.

4. Descending melodies offer more possibilities than ascending ones, since the normal resolution of the dominant seventh (or even ninth) is downward, a fact that requires constant supervision. To illustrate dominant embellishments, the second phrase of "Annie Laurie" might be varied as in Example 6.

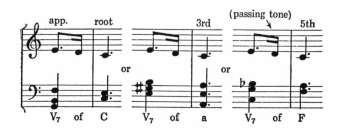

EXAMPLE 6

These generalized procedures represent the harmonic limits most pianists are likely to reach or need to reach insofar as playing by ear may affect the success of performance. Idiomatic progressions, like the passing six-four and four-three chords or the special handlings of the leading tone, are readily learned, but they apply much more to four-part harmonizations of the chorale type. The same is true of modulations, such as the approach to the bass of the I_4^6 chord in the new key through the diminished-seventh chord a half-step below, which is useful chiefly in improvisation.

Transposition to any and every key should figure as an integral part of all playing by ear. Fortunately, many beginners are required to play their early pieces in at least half a dozen keys. To be sure, this practice will not assure them of the skill that enabled

Brahms to transpose the piano part of Beethoven's "Kreutzer" Sonata from A to A-sharp at a moment's notice. But it will help them to sense inherent musical relationships and not just the mechanics of a single arrangement of notes on the keyboard. Incidentally, one American college now expects its recitalists to be ready to transpose at least one piece to any other key that is requested, right at the program!

The student will do well to keep a dated record of what he has played by ear each week, listing title and key and noting any difficulties that have arisen so that they can be discussed with the teacher—also so that he may realize which keys need the most attention.

Sight-Reading for Profit and Pleasure

Much is to be gained by regular sight-reading. First of all, there are the obvious advantages of being able to read fluently at sight. Fluency in this skill is a prime requisite of the professional pianist, especially of the accompanist, teacher, ensemble player, and radio and television staff member. It gives the student a chance to learn a new piece before he tires of it. Besides, nothing is likely to discourage him more than an initial struggle with a maze of incomprehensible notes—notes that may actually present no technical problem once he has learned to read them. Fluency, in other words, helps to make the piano study more pleasurable. And, to put it mildly, the matter of pleasure in music must not be overlooked! Sometimes we get so serious, even anxious, about our music study that we forget one of its main values, which is, after all, the pleasure music can afford.

A second main value of improved sight-reading is the readier access it gives to a wide variety of basic literature, both original and arranged, that the student otherwise might not get time to know. The poor sight-reader barely has time to keep up with the study and performance of the relatively limited repertoire in his

regular assignments. The good sight-reader, often reaching out on his own initiative, has an open door to a much broader acquaintance with music.

Finally, extensive sight-reading is sure to introduce a wealth of new technical, stylistic, and interpretative experiences that will contribute directly to the artistic and physical grasp of the pieces selected for more formal study. These wider experiences add perspective to whatever the student undertakes. Thanks to them, he studies his particular sonata or fugue not in isolation but in relation to a whole literature of sonatas or fugues.

Sight-reading should be gone at systematically, with a panorama of literature mapped out in advance. Naturally, while he is just starting, the student must content himself with persistent reading from his own and other beginners' books. Sight-reading of much elementary material should be a main ingredient in his early training, anyway. (See the discussion of the sight-reading approach early in Chapter 7.) After about a year he will be able to look into the easiest of the classics—the little preludes, sonatinas, and other short pieces that the great composers were thoughtful enough to leave to us. Eventually, he may begin to go through the standard literature—the Beethoven sonatas, the Bach "forty-eight," the Debussy preludes, the late pieces of Brahms, and all those other masterpieces that constitute the pianist's daily bread. Taking this approach, the student who can perform, say, the *Grande Sonate pathétique* of Beethoven may be expected to cover virtually the entire standard literature in as little as four years, with only a few minutes of reading a day. His chief problem, if he cannot afford to buy much of this music for himself, will be to find a library from which he can borrow. (See the discussion of this problem on page 28.)

The student should work through one complete volume before going on to the next, choosing according to the limitations of his technique and musical understanding, transferring from one era and style to another for variety and a balanced diet, and keeping a dated record of what he plays. As suggested above, if he is studying a Mozart sonata, a Chopin prelude, or any other piece that is one among many of its kind, he can extend his general perspective and his understanding of that piece by reading all of its fellows in the same volume.

He will profit still further if he undertakes to write brief but careful comments in a sight-reading notebook. He might start with concise personal reactions to each piece he reads. His object will be not merely to jot down, "It's pretty," or, "I don't like it," but to record what he would want especially to study in the future. The more he himself can be drawn into questions like the choice of repertoire the greater his interest is sure to be.

In addition, the student should take advantage of his sight-reading adventures to sharpen his critical wits. He can start in that direction by singling out, objectively and within his limitations, those traits that distinguish one piece from any other. For example, in what ways—melodic, rhythmic, harmonic, dynamic, textural, formal, technical, or other—does Schumann's *Carnaval* differ from his *Symphonic Etudes*, or, to take a more extreme example, how does Debussy's "Maid with the Flaxen Hair" differ from Handel's "Harmonious Blacksmith"? If he can but discern the basic structural difference (motivic reiteration as against variation treatment) between the two Schumann works, or the difference in harmonic color between the music of Debussy and Handel, he will have made important observations of his own. Moreover, just realizing that he must have something to jot down after he completes his reading compels him to be more consciously observant along the way.

Pianists do need to sharpen their critical wits. As is well known, with everything laid out literally in black and white before them, they can run on quite oblivious of the music they are playing. So can other instrumentalists, for that matter, though most of these must consider options in tone and pitch—options unavailable to the pianist—that promote more awareness at least of the performance if not of the content of the music. The violinist must consider options in pitch, for example, because his fingerboard has no frets to predetermine the pitch. Of course, all players of wind and bowed-stringed instruments have further options unavailable to the pianist that promote awareness, one being that of swelling, diminishing, or sustaining a tone at will.

A few suggestions should prove useful regarding the technique of sight-reading. The prime difficulty in sight-reading is rhythm more often than notes. Although there are eighty-eight notes on today's standard piano keyboard, combined in a nearly inexhaustible variety of harmonies, counterpoints, and dissonances, the notes can appear only in fixed places on the staff and on the keyboard. Rhythm, on the other hand, is much less predictable. To be sure, the number of different note values and signs in common use is not so great. But these occur, except in the most stereotyped dances, marches, and the like, in ever-changing combinations that cannot be foreseen—in fact, that are often meant to do the unexpected.

The performer has to do more than read rhythms; he has to sense them inwardly and in advance in order to understand and play them properly. It is at once evident that accurate counting is a *sine qua non* of sight-reading wherever there can be any possibility of confusion. Sight-reading should be done at a tempo that permits at least four-fifths of the notes to be played correctly. It also must be done musically, reproducing as nearly as possible the intention of the composer. Therefore, if getting in four-fifths of the notes means playing too slowly for the intent of the music, the student will have to read easier music until his skill improves. Naturally, the level of technique sets an upper limit.

Reading notes rapidly presents many of the same problems as reading words rapidly. Much of the reason "why Johnny can't read" is his inability (or lack of training) to perceive combinations of letters as syllables, combinations of syllables as words, and even combinations of words as whole phrases. Does he read *c-o-m-b-i-n-a-t-i-o-n-s,* or *com-bi-na-tions,* or *combinations?* Similarly, Johnny can be hindered in music reading by an inability to perceive combinations of notes as chords and combinations of chords as familiar progressions. Then he needs to develop a better command of harmony, both intuitive and intellectual, which he can do first of all by learning to play by ear. (One can begin to see how sight-reading actually can become an approach to piano study, again as discussed in our final chapter.) It is no wonder that the more unfamiliar the idiom is, like today's avant-garde music or an essay in a foreign language, the slower the sight-reading proves to be, whether of music notation or words.

Assuming the student is able to perceive tones and chords in intelligible combinations (or harmonic relationships), there are four main procedures that will advance his skill and confidence in sight-reading. The first is simply to read both a lot and a wide variety of piano music, as has already been advocated earlier in this section. In other words, the first prescription for learning to sight-read is to sight-read. The second procedure is to keep the eyes on the music, even during leaps. The sight-reader loses not only time but also his place in the score when he has to keep looking down to locate his hands on the keyboard. (Furthermore, feeling instead of looking for the keys has advantages to tone and technique, as discussed in later chapters.) One can break the habit of looking down by propping the keyboard cover over the hands just high enough to allow free movement yet still hide the keys from view. The third procedure is to take in as much of the notation as possible at a glance, recalling how a child learns to recognize whole words and even sentences from flash cards or how a military flyer learns to identify different planes or groups of planes from a fleeting glimpse of a photograph. The fourth procedure, closely related, is to look ahead *deliberately* in the score.

The sight-reader appreciates the problem of deliberately looking ahead only after he can get someone else to keep covering each measure while it is being played. Here Mr. Loesser inserts:

> Of course. In fact, I often say, "In music you must never think of what you are doing." Startled query: "Well, what *must* you think of?" Answer: "What you are *going* to do."

Actually, to look ahead the sight-reader will be doing two things at once—recording mentally what is coming while playing *from memory* what was previously recorded mentally. If the student thinks that such multiple activity is impossible, show him otherwise with a related procedure. Play the leading voice of any canon (such as the first main theme in the finale of Franck's Sonata for Piano and Violin) and *while that continues* get him to whistle or sing the imitating voice at the proper time interval. In other words, get him to hear what is coming *while* he reproduces what has passed. (You can make a similar, still easier demonstration by reading aloud from this or a like text and *while that continues* getting the student to repeat it almost at once.)

Sometimes the visual reaction speed can be improved by setting the metronome to the proper tempo and then sticking with it, come hell or high water. The use of the metronome in this way may induce a degree of "faking." But actually, a degree of faking, if it is the intelligent kind that depends on perceiving harmonic outlines and omitting only relatively unessential tones, is an important part of successful sight-reading, as any professional will readily confess. Sight-reading in ensemble music achieves the same results even better than the metronome, both because the players feel even more impelled to go on (the violinist in an orchestra must hang on for dear life because he knows the orchestra will never go back for him if he alone gets lost) and because they can be more musical when the rhythm is not hidebound by a metronome. And that brings us to another important developer of musicianship, ensemble playing.

Join an Ensemble and Be Musical

The pianist who has thus far failed to play in ensembles truly does not know how much pleasure he has missed. It would be no exaggeration to say that most experienced pianists find greater musical enjoyment in ensemble than in solo playing. This observation brings up both the pleasure and social values of music again. Ensemble playing is usually so much fun, socially as well as musically, that once the habit is set the student rarely needs any further inducements to keep it up. Since music does thrive in society, breaking the ice is about the only obstacle to getting students interested. Inertia has to be surmounted in the matters of making appointments to meet, finding a place to rehearse, and borrowing scores and parts. Often I have used part of the first studio recital by my students each semester to overcome this inertia. We have gathered at the ensemble shelves of the school library for first introductions to the music and to each other. Then I have stood right by until they committed themselves to definite appointments for four-hand duets at one or two pianos, in rooms known to be available at set times. When we have followed up these arrangements by crowding around two pianos to sample some pieces, the ice is broken and the interest aroused.

Piano duets are, of course, only one branch of ensemble playing. But, where instrumentalists other than pianists are scarce, duets

can go a long way toward meeting the needs of ensemble playing. Both the original music for four hands and the splendid standard arrangements should be played. It may surprise some to learn that Schubert's one-piano duets include works like the Grand Duo in C and the *Lebensstürme,* works that are quite as broadly conceived, as expressive, and as dramatic as his great Symphony in C and his two-cello Quintet in C. Indeed, to my mind, these are of more consistent worth and inspiration than much of his solo piano music. Similarly, I would put Mozart's great F major Sonata for one-piano duet and his sparkling D major Sonata for two pianos (as well, of course, as the piano concertos with the orchestra part reduced for second piano) quite on a par with his few finest solo sonatas.

Although the same cannot be said for the duets of Haydn, Beethoven, Schumann, or Mendelssohn, there are a number of other great works (more for one than for two pianos) to keep enterprising duettists occupied for a long while and to fill a number of exciting programs of original duets. There are, for example, the Variations Op. 23 by Brahms, the one- and two-piano sonatas by Hindemith, the delightful sonatas or suites by Kuhlau, Fauré, and

Debussy, and even some early Elizabethan music. Fortunately, there is good literature right from the beginning stage, thanks to venerable but still excellent series like that of Diller and Quaile, in which the pupil's part is made much easier than the teacher's.

As for arrangements, it is common knowledge that one of the best ways to explore the great masterpieces of chamber music and of the orchestra is through duet reductions. In their humble way, the excellent nineteenth-century arrangers, employed notably for Edition Peters, made an invaluable contribution when they thus supplied the best of all the great masters from Bach to Bruckner. In music schools, every effort should be made to stock the libraries with such arrangements.

If the pianist is to join with players on other instruments, the most common mediums will be the piano trio (piano, violin, and cello) and the duo for piano with one string or wind instrument. The original literature is similarly ample for these combinations and broad in the range of its difficulty. The arrangements are not so ample and are less likely to be of first-class quality. However, even the albums of hackneyed old favorites have their training value, be the piano parts ever so subordinate. The student will speak up soon enough if he is bored.

The importance of ensemble playing to sight-reading, to exploration of the classics, and to sheer musical pleasure has already been stressed. One other contribution, inherent in the very nature of this practice, has still to be stated. That is the sensitivity that ensemble playing awakens to musical values. This sensitivity results in large measure from the quick shifts of role that each player constantly must make in skillfully contrived ensemble music. Now he plays the accompaniment, now he takes the solo lead, now he drops out momentarily, and now he interchanges with the others as an equal partner. Such shifts quickly train him in the art of give-and-take, of knowing what should project and what should be subordinated.

Surprisingly, though loud playing seems to be congenital among pianists, the common fault of the novice in ensembles with other types of instruments (though not in piano duets) is to regard everything in the piano part as an accompaniment to be subdued. Even when the pianist does recognize a solo as such he often lacks the courage to assert his part. In his timidity he may not realize that modern chamber music grew out of compositions by Haydn, Mozart, and their forerunners in which the piano took the solo lead while the strings played subordinate parts almost exclusively. Even the "Kreutzer" Sonata by Beethoven was originally called a sonata for piano with violin obbligato! Nothing is quite so musically frustrating as to hear one of the fine "piano and violin" sonatas by Brahms played as though the piano had only an accompaniment, its part being at least as important as the violin's. To be sure, there is the other extreme. But I am simply passing by the brash pianist who drowns out his cohorts unmercifully or the well-meaning accompanist who tries to attach prime melodic significance to a purely harmonic background.

Much as for other performers, rhythm looms as the biggest challenge for ensemble players. This challenge is to be expected, of course, since the very act of playing together depends on rhythmic agreement. And as always, counting aloud and the use of the metronome are basic props, at least until the players manage to stay together. Even then the metronome may be a powerful aid in giving over-all continuity to the performance, as will be discussed later and as is well known to experienced chamber music organizations.

Music and Books—The Tools of the Profession

Under the general heading of musicianship one other topic must be included—that is, the importance to the developing student of collecting a basic library. This topic is appropriate to each of our seven chapters, but especially to this one, since the basic library furnishes a prime means of cultivating musicianship, just as it furnishes a fund of literature from which the pianist can draw the pieces he studies to perform, the pieces he plays for recreation, and the pieces he explores to extend his musical horizons. As soon as the student shows promise of continuing interest, he should be approached about the possibility of buying in one lump purchase those works that represent the cornerstones of piano literature—those works that would be essential to his musicianly pleasures were he to be stranded on the proverbial desert isle. Since a sizable cash outlay will be involved, his parents may need to be approached, too.

Several advantages accrue thereby to the student. First, he supplies himself at once with resources constantly at hand for future exploration, study, and beneficial enjoyment. These resources will be basic to him because they represent the greatest music for his instrument, the music that has continually influenced other musicians, and the music that is most often performed and cited. Second, the student may very well effect a major economy by buying this much music at once. There is the obvious fact that savings up to 300 and 400 per cent may be made by buying the complete volume of any one type of piece (for instance, all the twenty-seven Chopin etudes) rather than one at a time, as the need arises. But, in addition, there is the frequent possibility of a dealer discount for a purchase of this size.

Third, a rounded basic library helps to insure against conspicuous gaps in the student's repertoire. Of course, a careful teacher will make periodic checks to ascertain and eliminate those gaps, but the student's own explorations are still the best way of discovering them. Fourth, a rounded basic library also helps to insure against unbalanced tastes, such as a passion for Bartók and an aversion to Chopin, or vice versa. The dilettante appreciator may argue that he likes what he likes, but the career musician should be discouraged from this view. As a careerist, he should make it his business to understand and really like the best music of every era, or else find out wherein he, not the composer, is lacking.

Finally, the student who makes such a lump purchase has an opportunity and an inclination to choose with care the editions he gets. Editions that are inaccurate, badly reproduced, or unwisely marked can both discourage and harm him. Each edition must be evaluated separately, since bad as well as good editions appear in the catalogues of almost all publishers. The pronounced swing toward *Urtext* editions—that is, editions in which the music has been reproduced exactly as the composer left it, with any additions bracketed or otherwise identified—is a healthy sign. However, that swing may have gone too far from the student's standpoint. For example, I would almost rather entrust my students to the old Bülow-Lebert edition of Beethoven's sonatas than to the *Urtext,* in which Beethoven's inconsistencies, especially in the matter of staccatos, slurs, and dynamic signs, can produce no end of confusion—almost rather, that is, because the Bülow-Lebert edition, although a true labor of love, went too far the other way, not only inserting numerous unidentified changes but also making various details consistent that were never meant to be.

The Bach *Urtext* editions are a little easier to use, since Bach inserted virtually no editorial markings in his keyboard music, thus giving less occasion for such inconsistencies. Even so, much experience with Bach is needed to surmise unaided his probable intentions with regard to tempo, articulation, dynamics, expressive freedom, and other stylistic problems. To take the most familiar problem, in Bach's keyboard music as in nearly all keyboard music from William Byrd to Beethoven and even Chopin, decisions are needed continually with regard to appropriate realizations of the ornament signs. The student is encouraged later in this book to do some of his own investigating of ornaments. But certainly in this problem, as in the others, the authoritative, up-to-date advice of a fully qualified editor is needed. The ornament solutions in some of the older standard editions, and in some of the newer ones, too, are among their worst misrepresentations, providing one example after another that the well-meaning student will only have to un-learn later.

There follows a suggested list for a pianist's basic library, with one or more recommended editions, generally in order of prefer-ence, for each main item. It would be tempting to add further standard masterworks by the same and other composers. Par-ticularly for the Modern Era—even though we do not yet know what will survive as "standard masterworks"—it would be tempt-ing to add representative compositions by men like Scriabin, Ravel, Milhaud, Hindemith, Prokofiev, and Schoenberg, as well as Ives and Copland in this country. (Teachers will want to see the new annotated bibliography of contemporary teaching pieces by Stanley Butler, listed in the Source References.) But then, if the four eras are to be kept in balance, our list would expand quickly in every direction beyond practical limits. The two books at the head of the list deal respectively with subject matter in music and with com-posers; they are currently the most practical and authoritative of their types published in English. The music is subdivided chrono-logically according to "The Four Main Eras of Keyboard Music" described on pages 167–168, permitting the student to keep balancing his musical diet.

The whole of this solo list, in the least expensive of the editions recommended, may be had for approximately $250, as of this writing (1974). Needless to say, the teacher will do best not to try to serve as a go-between but rather to furnish a choice of at least two or three dealers so that the student or parent can negotiate directly. (Here is the place to caution against those graded, "progressive" courses of study or those "complete libraries" that the parent or teacher all too often is pressured into ordering in advance on a contractual basis. Even if the editions and their pedagogic advice were acceptable, which I have never known them to be, the idea of prescribing treatments before the needs are known seems preposterous; it negates the custom-made instruction that is taken for granted in private lessons.) Readers in and about the largest cities, especially New York, Boston, Philadelphia, Chicago, and Los Angeles, should not overlook the possibility of getting standard music and music books in good used condition at one of the numerous cut-rate "music exchanges." Incidentally, the procurement of this much music gives a good opportunity to show the student how to care for it properly. He would do well to provide covers for it, house it in organized fashion, and even maintain a catalogue file of what he has. He should also be warned that the loss of music may mean much more than the cost of replacement. It may mean the loss of hard-won fingerings and other personal markings that can be invaluable when he wants to relearn a piece.

A SELECTED BASIC LIBRARY OF BOOKS AND MUSIC FOR PIANISTS

BOOKS

Willi Apel, *Harvard Dictionary of Music*, 2d ed. Cambridge, Mass.: Harvard University Press, 1969 or later.

Baker's Biographical Dictionary of Musicians, 5th or later ed., with latest supplement. New York: G. Schirmer, 1971 or later.

(Further books are recommended in the Source References on pages 200–203, including two extended bibliographies prepared by Maurice Hinson, one listing books for pianists and the other, music. These last can be of much help during the further building of the library. Also, every studio of serious piano instruction should be equipped with *Grove's Dictionary of Music and Musicians,* the completely new 6th edition of which is scheduled to appear from Macmillan of London in 1976.)

BAROQUE KEYBOARD MUSIC (about 1580–1750)

The Fitzwilliam Virginal Book (compiled around 1620). Edited by J. A. Fuller-Maitland and W. Squire for Breitkopf & Härtel and reprinted by Dover. 2 vols. A prime (low-cost) treasure of nearly 300 pieces by such contemporaries of Shakespeare as Bull, Byrd, Gibbons, and Farnaby.

François Couperin ("le Grand"; 1668–1733): at least a representative collection, such as the second of the 4 volumes ("livres de pièces de clavecin") that contain his 27 suites ("ordres") as edited by K. Gilbert for Heugel (in Le Pupitre series), or the anthology edited by Helmut Schultz for Edition Peters (4407c).

Domenico Scarlatti (1685–1757): at least a representative collection, such as any of the 11 volumes of the "complete" 545 sonatas being edited by K. Gilbert for Heugel (in Le Pupitre series), or the first volume (including the 30 "Essercizi per gravicembalo") of the 18 volumes containing facsimiles of early printed and manuscript sources as edited by R. Kirkpatrick for Johnson Reprint, or the *Sixty Sonatas* in 2 volumes edited by R. Kirkpatrick for G. Schirmer, or the *Sixty* (most played) *Sonatas* in an *Urtext* of early sources published by Breitkopf & Härtel and reprinted by Kalmus.

Johann Sebastian Bach (1685–1750): (15 two-part) *Inventions and* (15 three-part) *Sinfonias, French Suites, English Suites, Partitas, Well-Tempered Clavier, Toccatas, Concerto in F Minor.* The preferred edition should become the complete Bach *Neue Ausgabe* from Bärenreiter as each volume in Series V (keyboard) appears, under G. v. Dadelesen's editorship. Also especially recommended are the editions of W. Lampe for Henle; L. Landshoff, A. Kreutz, and K. Soldan for Peters; and H. Bischoff for Steingräber (reprinted today by Kalmus).

Georg Friedrich Handel (1685–1759): 16 *Suites* in 2 or 3 volumes, 6 "grandes" *Fugues*. Edited variously by R. Steglich and P. Northway for the *Hallische Händel-Ausgabe* (Bärenreiter), W. Serauky for Peters, and F. Chrysander for Breitkopf & Härtel (reprinted today by Kalmus).

CLASSIC KEYBOARD MUSIC (about 1730–1830)

Joseph Haydn (1732–1809): up to 54 complete extant sonatas in 3 to 5 volumes; sets of variations and other, shorter pieces. Edited variously by C. Landon for Universal, G. Feder and S. Gerlach for the Haydn-Institut (Henle), and C. A. Martienssen and K. Soldan for Peters.

Wolfgang Amadeus Mozart (1756–1791): up to 21 sonatas in 1 or 2 volumes; 14 fantasies, rondos, and other shorter pieces. The preferred edition should become that of the complete Mozart *Neue Ausgabe* from Bärenreiter as the remaining volumes appear in Series IX (keyboard). Also recommended are the editions by N. Broder for Presser *(Sonatas and Fantasies)*, W. Weismann for Peters *(Piano Pieces),* and W. Lampe for Henle *(Sonatas)*.

Ludwig van Beethoven (1770–1827): up to 38 sonatas in 2 to 5 volumes; up to 22 sets of variations in 1 or 2 volumes; a representative collection of the bagatelles, rondos, dances, and other shorter pieces. The preferred edition should become the new *Complete Edition of Beethoven's Works* from Henle as each volume in Series VII (piano) appears, under the editorship of H. Schmidt, J. Schmidt-Görg, and others. Also especially recommended are the editions of the sonatas by B. Wallner for Henle, H. Schenker and E. Ratz for Universal, H. Unverricht for Universal (in progress), and C. Arrau and L. Hoffmann-Erbrecht for Peters (in progress).

ROMANTIC PIANO MUSIC (about 1790–1915)

Franz Schubert (1797–1828): up to 12 complete sonatas in 1 or 2 volumes; a collection of the Fantasias, Impromptus, and *Moments musicaux*. The preferred edition should become the complete Schubert *Neue Ausgabe* from Bärenreiter as each volume in Series VII (piano) appears. Also especially recommended are the editions of P. Mies for Henle (sonatas), E. Ratz for Universal (sonatas), and P. Badura-Skoda for Universal (shorter pieces).

Felix Mendelssohn (1809–1847): Piano Works in 4 volumes (among them Etudes, Variations, Preludes and Fugues, Scherzos, and *Songs Without Words*). Edited by T. Kullak for Peters and J. Reitz for Breitkopf & Härtel (reprinted by Kalmus).

Frédéric Chopin (1810–1849): Ballades, Etudes, Impromptus, Mazurkas, Nocturnes, Polonaises, Preludes, Scherzos and Fantasy, Sonatas, and Waltzes. The preferred editions today are those from Henle (in progress by various editors, including separate volumes of annotations) and from the Fryderyk Chopin Institute in Warsaw (edited chiefly by L. Bronarski and J. Turczyński). A new "complete" critical edition has been projected by Polskie Wydawn in Cracow, starting with Jan Ekier's edition of the Ballades in 1967.

Robert Schumann (1810–1856): Piano Works in several volumes (among them *Carnaval, Fantasy Pieces, Forest Scenes, Papillons, Kreisleriana,* 3 Sonatas, *Scenes from Childhood,* and *Symphonic Etudes*). The two preferred editions, as the volumes continue to appear, should become the pertinent volumes in the new complete works projected by the Robert Schumann Society since 1964 by Breitkopf & Härtel and Schott, and the *Piano Solos* as edited by O. v. Irmer and W. Lampe for Henle. Clara Schumann's somewhat personal edition of the Complete Works for Piano Solo in 6 volumes has been reprinted by Kalmus.

Franz Liszt (1811–1886): Piano Works in several volumes (among them the Hungarian Rhapsodies, Etudes, *Liebestraüme,* Consolations, Sonata, (3) *Années de Pèlerinage,* and opera transcriptions). The preferred edition should become the pertinent volumes, edited thus far by Z. Gardonyi and I. Szelenyi, as they appear in the new complete works from Bärenreiter and Editio Musica Budapest. Until then, Peters, Kalmus, and G. Schirmer are the sources for the standard editions of Sauer, Friedheim, Busoni, Jossefy, Pauer, and others.

Johannes Brahms (1833–1897): Piano Works in two volumes (among them the Sonatas, Variations, *Balladen, Intermezzi, Capricci,* and *Rhapsodien*), as edited by E. Mandyczewski for Breitkopf & Härtel (reprinted by G. Schirmer); also, by E. Sauer (Peters and Kalmus).

MODERN PIANO MUSIC (since about 1890)

Claude Debussy (1862–1918): *Deux Arabesques,* (suite) *Pour le piano, Estampes, Images* (both sets), *Children's Corner, Préludes* (both books), and *Douze Etudes;* as published originally by Durand or Jobert.

Béla Bartók (1881–1945): *Fourteen Bagatelles, Ten Easy Piano Pieces, For Children* (2 volumes), *Fifteen Hungarian Peasant Songs and Dances,* (6) *Rumanian Folk Dances, Suite* (Op. 14), Sonata, (suite) *Out of Doors, Mikrokosmos* (at least volumes 5 and 6); as published primarily by Boosey & Hawkes.

ADDITIONAL RECOMMENDATIONS

Any expansions of the foregoing list would be likely soon to add the other composers cited in the capsule descriptions of "The Four Main Eras of Keyboard Music" on pages 167–168, especially the Modern Era. But the student will also want his "Basic Library" to include some of the main ensemble music with piano—first, some of the four-hand masterworks for one or two pianos such as were suggested earlier in this chapter; then, some of the great duos and trios with violin, cello, or other solo instrument(s) by the "three Bs" and other leading creators of chamber music; and ultimately, at least a representation of the most successful concertos for piano with orchestra by Mozart, Beethoven, Mendelssohn, Chopin, Schumann, Brahms, Tchaikovsky, Grieg, Rachmaninov, Prokofiev, and Bartók. (Since the orchestra part is usually arranged for a second piano in one superimposed score, it is naturally better if two copies of each concerto can be procured.)

Finally, one hopes the enterprising pianist will want to extend his library beyond the keyboard to some of those bibles of music literature that every roundly educated musician should know, such as Bach's 371 *Harmonized Chorales* and his *St. Matthew Passion,* Beethoven's nine symphonies and his *Missa Solemnis,* Brahms's *German Requiem,* Mozart's *Don Giovanni,* Wagner's *Tristan und Isolde,* and Verdi's *Otello.* (It is easiest, of course, to read through the symphonies in duet reductions and the vocal works in piano-vocal scores.) Pianists who value authenticity and a sense of greater closeness to the composer will enjoy acquiring some of the facsimiles of early sources that have become available at reasonable prices. Thus, they might get Book I of *The Well-Tempered Clavier* (Deutscher Verlag für Musik, in Leipzig) and the complete *Inventionen und Sinfonien* (Peters or Dover) in Bach's own hand, or one boxed set containing not only the autograph but the original printed edition of Beethoven's "Moonlight" Sonata and another set containing the same of his "Appassionata" Sonata (both sets published by Ongaku No Tomasha, in Tokyo), or the *Twenty-four Preludes* as well as other autographs by Chopin (The Fryderyk Chopin Institute, in Warsaw).

2. Technique:
The Basic Mechanisms

TECHNIQUE IS CONSIDERED in this chapter mainly in its more limited sense of physical agility. That is the sense usually intended by the earthy colloquialism "he plays a lot of piano." The desire for a "big" and fluent technique has occasioned so much discussion

and consumed so much time and energy that any further mention of the subject must be approached with trepidation. Yet, paradoxically, it is precisely that flood of attention that underlies some of the chief remarks to be made here. Sometimes, when the accumulation of material about any topic has been too great—as was the problem when Ernest Newman wrote about Wagner, or Hindemith about written harmony—the best new contribution is a reconsideration of the evidence, a sloughing off of excess verbiage, and a righting of false notions.

A first, practical consideration in any discussion of technique should be physical capabilities and limitations. Do we bear these in mind when we plan our courses of study? Not sufficiently. Just as a person will dress so as to draw attention to his more attractive features and away from any less attractive ones, so every pianist must take stock of himself, make the most of what he has, and try not to run afoul of his shortcomings. Make no mistake about this—every pianist has shortcomings, if only because the physical advantage that makes one passage easy is often the disadvantage that makes another hard. For example, long fingers frequently help in wide stretches but get in their own way in close, chromatic passages.

In any case, we must realize that we have to get along with the equipment that was given us. Fortunately, the literature for piano, unlike that for more specialized solo instruments like viola or oboe, is so extensive that one can usually select programs within his technical limitations and still not compromise his individual tastes. Natural bodily grace, the general nervous structure, the size and shape of the hand, the length and web of the fingers, "breaking" at the finger joints, and general pliability—any or all of these may vary widely and represent some of the most important differences between one person's technical capabilities and another's.

My own impression has come to be that the hand with the most advantages, and the one that achieves the greatest technical wizardry with the least effort, is the chubby, pliable, square hand of moderate size and finger lengths. (Schubert's reported facility at the keyboard, with little training, and his nickname of "Schwammerl," or "Tubby," come to mind!) In any case, those differences from one hand to the next can be intriguing, as I learned through a series of inquiries into the pianist's anatomy (see Nos. 36, 64, and 76 of the *Piano Quarterly*). The extreme variability of the hand structure and the incompetence of most of us pianists to pronounce on matters physiological were but two of the findings.

Among others, for example, it appears that the fourth finger is linked and subordinate to the fifth as often as to the third finger in different hands. It also appears that most men have longer fourth than second fingers, and most women the converse (which circumstance can affect, among other things, chord fingerings). And it turns out that the uncertain stories about Schumann's celebrated hand injury reduce to a congenital weakness of the second and third fingers on his right hand, augmented to the point of near paralysis by his tying those fingers back for periods of time on the mistaken theory that he was thus strengthening them.

Carl Seashore, best known for his widely used tests of musical talent, also developed a motor test for measuring technical capability. It records the number of times the hand can tap per second and, like the talent tests, purports to apply equally to all persons whether they have had musical training or not. Even to the extent that this ability can be measured by eye and ear alone, I have noted among my students a marked correlation between tapping speed and technical fluency. Of course, there is no denying the importance of other factors in the building of a secure technique, too. Technical capability is hardly synonymous with technical achievement, which requires, besides the good hand, an intelligent approach to technical problems, a perception of technical fluency as a musical need, and the usual perspiration that figures in all such achievement.

About Sitting and Hand Positions

Both sensible and salutary is the current widespread reaction against those outworn, hard-and-fast "methods" of piano playing that call for fixed, sometimes rigid, positions and uniform attacks in all situations. In the first place, those methods fix the performer so primly and properly that we almost expect the piano to come to him. Certainly, they help him but little to adapt himself to the multiform requirements of the piano. If anything, they interfere

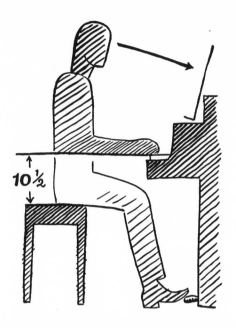

10½

with the constant adjustments and extensions, both lateral and vertical, that must be made in order to work in and out of the black and white keys with short and long fingers. The use of a lowered wrist, with fingers neatly rounded and knuckles held in, may recall pictures of the young Mozart or resemble Iturbi's position as seen in the movies, but that position hardly becomes the ideal for all pianists or all music.

The real ideals of position are pliability, adaptability, and that sort of easy yet alert posture that comes halfway between a rigid and a slumped position. The average student who is healthy and normally graceful needs but little instruction to fall into good habits of posture. Often when he attacks the piano awkwardly, there are other factors responsible. The most common factor is the use of a bench that is too high or too low. Since the height of the piano itself varies considerably, the best measure is the distance from the surface of the keys (that is, the ivories) down to the compressed top of the bench. About ten inches is normal. Very short persons or persons with short arms may prefer to lessen that distance by as much as an inch. Sitting too low, which is perhaps the worse of the two evils, constrains the finger action by raising the wrists and knuckles; sitting too high constrains the hand action by lowering the wrists and elbows. Another factor affecting position is bad eyesight, which often causes the performer to edge closer and closer to the piano in order to read his music. The adjustable music rack on most grand pianos usually lessens this problem.

A few further recommendations regarding position will suffice here, along with the reminder that individual differences may justify surprising variations. It is best to sit only on the front half of the bench; covering the whole bench induces slumping. The edge of the knees should be not more than an inch or two under the keyboard. In this position, which will seem far out to some, the body is alert for action, both rhythmic and athletic. Moreover, the arms and shoulders have full freedom and the wrist action is not cramped. Every once in a while students need to extend their arms sideways and rotate them vigorously from their shoulders, both clockwise and counterclockwise. Then they will remember that they do have shoulders and they will emerge from those constricted, almost strait-jacketed positions in which they too often sit.

The balls of the feet should rest on the "balls" of the outer pedals, ready to pedal at a moment's notice. Intertwining the feet around the bench legs not only interferes with ready pedaling but causes the back to slump and thus lessens endurance in long practice. In fact, the legs, arms, and back work somewhat as a unit. Their improper alignment leads to early fatigue and faulty hand action, as is suggested in the diagram on page 42. The performance of octaves, in particular, requires that the performer be firmly planted.

The elbows usually will need to be several inches out from the body. Putting them out helps to compensate for the unequal finger lengths, especially for the short fifth finger. Pressing them against the body constrains the arm, forearm, and hand action. Moreover, only when the elbows stand out from the body a few inches do the hands lie flat without effort over the keyboard. The further the elbows move out or in, the more the hands want to follow them, and the more constraining and tiring becomes the effort to keep them flat.

The elbow tips will usually be on a level with the fingertips if the performer is sitting at the right height. Though the middle of the keyboard comes between e′ and f′, most players prefer to sit in front of—that is, with their nose on a vertical line with—middle C or d′. Finger, hand, and arm positions vary with the type of technique, as discussed presently. The student will profit by watching himself in a mirror now and then as he plays, noting in particular the items just mentioned. For that matter, the teacher, who is accustomed to giving all his lessons from one viewpoint in the studio, will be surprised at the new concept he may get of the student's playing position by moving to the other side of him.

The player who leans far to the left or right to play passages in the extreme ranges should bear in mind that he is upsetting the support for his aim. He is taxing himself somewhat as a gunner would who attempts to shoot on the run. Furthermore, by moving his arms and body as a single unit he sacrifices a desirable freedom at the shoulders. Later we shall be trying some exercises in contrary motion from the center to the extreme ends of the keyboard that can help to correct this fault when it becomes a problem.

The Four Main Playing Mechanisms

It is common knowledge that most playing is done by the finger working from the knuckle at its base, or the hand from the wrist, or the forearm from the elbow, or the upper arm from the shoulder. The useful application of this knowledge through further deductions is not so common. First, some general points

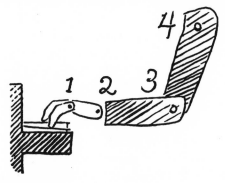

should be made. These four mechanisms are sometimes used separately, sometimes in various combinations. So that any one of them may be specified where needed or avoided where not, the student should first learn to use each mechanism by itself. He might do this, for example, by practicing each one in turn, each hand alone, on the five white keys leading outward from middle C and back.

If he understands how all four mechanisms are based on much the same leverage principle, he will be able to control them better. Unfortunately, nothing else in piano pedagogy has engendered quite so much hokum as the musculature, anatomy, and mechanics of piano technique. Especially at the elementary level, as in the gratuitous comments to be found in many a first-year method, one is instructed with a great show of authority to apply all manner of absurd curatives—for example, to "rotate the elbow" in this passage, to "loosen the wrist" in that one, or to "play with soft fingertips" in yet another! (For more examples, see the *Piano Quarterly* No. 29, pp. 29–30.) Or one reads, in countless variants, about elaborate up-down motions and other aerial acrobatics that occur quite outside the sphere of the keyboard itself. It is partly to cut through such hokum that the basic leverage principle is restated and developed here.

In more explicit terms, then, how does the leverage principle relate to those four human mechanisms under discussion? The lever itself is the finger, or the hand, or the forearm, or the upper—that is, full—arm. Its fulcrum, or hinge, is the knuckle, wrist, elbow, or shoulder, respectively. The stationary base for the fulcrum is *everything beyond it,* starting with the hand as the base for the knuckle, the forearm for the wrist, the upper arm for the elbow, and the trunk for the shoulder. The force comes from muscles imbedded in the base, which mostly work the levers up or down through (inflexible) tendons. And the object of the force is always—for our purposes, of course—the key. (The foregoing diagram should suffice. But those seeking to explore the mechanics of leverage still further might start with the diagram under "lever" in most standard dictionaries, our type being the "third class" inverted.) A fifth lever that we shall meet, also valuable though less used in piano playing, is the trunk, its fulcrum being the hips and its base the lower body.

Two interrelated points about the use of the levers need to be made at once, for their neglect or misunderstanding accounts for much faulty playing and misguided effort. The ideal of technical efficiency, assuming it satisfies the musical need, occurs (1) when the base of the lever does remain stationary, and (2) when only one lever is used at a time. Departing from the ideal in either respect means both harder work and less control (or predictability).

Thus, to allow the base to give way to the force you exert on the lever is like using a foam-rubber mattress to stand on when you shove your piano to another spot. You not only work harder (to play the key or shove the piano) but you also lose control because you cannot predict how much of your effort will be wasted and how much will take effect. Any give in the base will have the same effect whether it is in the hand just beyond the knuckle, or the arm, or the trunk, or the bench, or the floor, and so on all the way down to mother earth. A complete loss of support means no leverage effect at all. In other words, the pianist who fails to "fix" the base sufficiently to withstand the lever action simply abandons that lever and transfers the responsibility to the next or even the next lever, since eventually *some* base *some*where along the line must be fixed enough to enable the lever to strike and to release the key. The result again is increasing work and decreasing control. Musically, one of the most characteristic results is the nondescript arm jogging described shortly under the (intended) use of the fingers.

As for using more than one mechanism at a time, the problem is the increasing complexity of the control. A man standing still in a shooting gallery with only a stationary clay pigeon to get in his sights has only one factor to consider. But as additional factors enter in—a movement of the pigeon from left to right, a breeze that deflects it from above, a treadmill that revolves under the man's feet from front to back—he soon gets beyond hope of any precise aim and must trust more and more to chance. The arm jogging just mentioned also results from too many mechanisms, which are forced into play as each further base is abandoned. However, please note that certain combination touches, to be described presently, do have their special justifications, mainly in the interests of strength and endurance.

Let us return, then, to the learning of one touch or mechanism at a time. As the student practices each successive lever—from finger, to hand, to forearm, to upper arm—he not only must watch that the base beyond remains stationary each time, but he must also take increasing pains to keep each lever intact as a single locked unit. For example, when the upper arm is the lever, there must be no give anywhere along the line from shoulders to fingertips—no break, that is, at the elbow, wrist, or any of the other intervening hinges. Otherwise, that battle against overwork and undercontrol has been lost again. Breaking at the intervening hinges is simply another way to arrive at more than one mechanism at a time. To help get a feel for each touch alone the student should try working the finger (or other lever) throughout the full orbit of motion that its knuckle (or other hinge) permits, although his eventual ideal will be economy of motion. To help insure that the base remains stationary, the student should try applying the middle finger of his other hand as a kind of sensor, pressing it lightly just beyond the lever's hinge (as on the small of the wrist beyond the hand or the small of the shoulder beyond the upper arm).

Which touch to use must depend, of course, on the musical need in any one situation. Eventually one reacts intuitively to that need, without having to decide consciously which touch will best suit each change of style. But at first the student will profit by doing a deliberate touch analysis of each new piece he sets out to learn (similar to the analyses on pages 181–182 of three pieces in different styles). In effect, he will be determining the best tool to do each job—the screwdriver to turn the screw, the hammer to strike the nail, and so on. Help comes from recognizing the inherent capabilities and limitations of the individual touch mechanisms themselves.

If the musical passage in question were entirely slow and simple enough, any touch or combination of touches might be made to do the work, including the trunk working from the hips. But, by and large, each touch does have its best uses. Thus, the fingers answer best for legato playing and for nearly all the single- or double-note playing, including the fastest playing, that does not require either detaching at slow to moderate speeds or leaping. The hands serve most readily for the playing of staccato at moderate speeds, as in octave passages. The forearm mainly provides the maximum source of power as well as accuracy for the playing of single tones, intervals, and chords that need to be emphasized, and for detached successions of these. It can also keep shifting the hand and fingers to different locations. And the upper, or full, arm fulfills three important kinds of missions: (1) to play the single tones, intervals, and chords, and the detached successions of these that do not require quite the forearm's power cum accuracy; (2) to act as the prime mover for the attacks and releases or the shifts to different keyboard locations of the other three touch mechanisms; and (3) to unite with any of these other mechanisms in the valuable combination touches shortly to be described.

Naturally, there is a tendency to oversimplify in such a basic listing of touch uses. The further cultivation of the touches becomes very complex and musically subtle. But the student needs to perceive first things first. And he also needs to understand certain relationships and differences between the touches. First, the fingers are the ideal means of legato because they enjoy almost exclusive rights to the *prepared attack,* which means starting from the surface of the keys. All the other touches depend primarily on *unprepared attacks* (from above the surface). Second, in most piano playing the fingers and hands do the lion's share of playing, but it is rare for the other touches not to contribute, at least in combinations. For instance, the fingers and hands suffice to make the precise distinctions between legato and staccato that help to identify the refined Mozart style, but the full arm (as a locked unit) needs to share in such further niceties of that style as sudden accents in the course of rapid passagework or drops on the start of each two-note slur in a stepwise series (as discussed later).

Third, only the forearm and upper arm can roll sideways from their hinges, along with the vertical and more or less horizontal movements that all four mechanisms can make. The sideways roll adds to the use of the forearm and upper arm in combination touches, as in the rotary motion to be mentioned shortly. Furthermore, three of the hinges—knuckle, wrist, and shoulder—are like ball joints in permitting almost complete rotation of their levers. But the elbow hinge is different, for it permits no such rotation (not to be confused with that sideways roll at the radio-ulnar joint). A notable result for pianists is the exceptional accuracy of the forearm once it is pointed in the right direction. (Try using the forearms, for example, to help guarantee the accuracy of those treacherous but innocent-looking octaves in the first solo entry of Beethoven's Third Piano Concerto, as reproduced in Example 7.)

EXAMPLE 7

Still another difference between the four touches is the wrist height most often advantageous to each. All other things being equal, a slightly low wrist is advantageous in the finger touch, especially when one employs the flatter finger action shortly to be considered. But in the other three mechanisms, a slightly high wrist is more likely to be advantageous. For example, when the hand is used to play octaves, starting with a low wrist would only mean that the hand's upward motion is already used up.

Finally, the student needs to understand how the four touches depend on an inverse ratio of speed to power. Much faulty playing and harsh sound will be spared by the constant reminder that an increase in speed must mean a sacrifice in power, and vice versa. The analogy of an automobile's four-speed stick shift can be illuminating, within limits. We use low or first gear (the upper arm) when maximum power rather than smooth speed is the first consideration. We use second gear (the forearm) when we still need extra power, but with a little more speed. We use third gear (the hand) when we want enough driving speed, though still with a degree of power available. And finally, we use high or top gear (the fingers) for that substantial part of the driving where maximum smooth speed and not power is the prime consideration. (One flaw in this analogy, of course, is the implication that the shoulder is a more usable source of power than the forearm.) Pianists need power mainly for loudness. Perhaps the main deduction to be made from this principle is the fact that too much power can be a nuisance. *For utmost efficiency we must use the least powerful mechanism that will answer the need.* When we are driving on the open highway we do not use low or second gear because (1) that would be a waste of power (power is a vital factor in piano endurance) and (2) that would delimit the speed. Both objections concern serious technical faults to be found in the playing of many earnest, hard-working students. They are further considered in the individual discussions of the four playing mechanisms that follow.

The Use of the Fingers

The first problem in teaching the use of the fingers is to get them actually into use. Once this is achieved, the matters of correct stroke and the special movement of the thumb may or may not have to be considered, depending upon the natural aptitudes of the student. Without instruction to the contrary, most students (as well as most pianists who are badly out of practice) do their playing by impulses from the arm, the fingers moving just enough so that the whole hand does not strike at once. In other words, these students fail to make that essential stationary base out of the hand, merely transferring the responsibility all the way back to the trunk. The result is a very common jogging or bouncing motion of the hand and arm, along with reduced speed and control. The speed, in fact, is limited to that of the arm jogging! The loss of control is most evident in a sacrifice of legato to detached playing.

Ignorance of finger action and laziness partly account for this fault. So do misguided efforts to exploit the weight of the arm. The familiar weight-of-the-arm prescription is very misleading. Obviously, to rest the arm's full weight or, as one alternative expression goes, to "relax completely" merely results in utter limpness and a collapse of the leverage principle. Moreover, in piano playing the popular remark about gravity must be reversed: what goes down must come up. It is an illusion to suppose that a continuous flow of weight stands ready to be poured from above, as it were. The more weight that is dropped, the more that must be lifted again and replaced. In short, we are back to the principle that advises the use of only as large a mechanism (for which read here, "only as much weight") as the music requires at any one time. The dropping of too much weight must mean unnecessary effort quite as much as a too rigid or tense support of unused weight means unnecessary effort.

Formerly, in slow music especially, the use of arm weight, rested upon a sufficiently braced finger, was regarded as an ideal means of producing a full, rounded, yet unforced tone. There seemed to be ample time to draw so heavy a mechanism back up again and, while still holding the key down to preserve the legato, transfer the weight to the next key. To be sure, as the speed increased, the pianist who tried to maintain the same weight would only wear himself down by exerting more and more effort until he was stopped, in any case, by his physical limitations. But more to the point here is the doubt as to whether dropping (if not plopping) weight can ever achieve the same control as deliberately placing it.

Another cause of arm jogging is the desire to play louder and sound bigger than the fingers alone will permit. This desire is at best a matter of taste but more often of inexperience. Overly loud playing has been widely condemned. Perhaps the loudness is only indicative of artistic trends in these tempestuous times. Personally, I hope not. I hope that the piano is not becoming more and more of a percussion instrument at the expense of its fine capabilities for lyricism and poetry, and at the expense of a very precious element in art, gentleness. However that may be, when the volume demanded is too great for the fingers, the other mechanisms involuntarily come into play. The other mechanisms are bigger and more powerful, and hence the speed is curtailed, as just explained. (Yet, according to one New York reviewer, already jaded at the start of a recent new season, "Well, the pianists are off again, [both] louder and faster than ever!") The control is curtailed, too, whether by the bulkier mechanisms or by their nondescript combination in a futile snakelike motion. Without a firm support or base for his finger action, the pianist is then in the position of a gardener who tries to weed with a rubber-handled hoe.

To correct this fault, the student might try the old stunt of balancing a penny on the back of each wrist while playing scales with both hands. The fatigue that comes from picking up the pennies a good many times acts like a sulphur-and-molasses cure. Another help is exaggerated raising of the fingers so that each one strikes like a little metallic hammer and pops back the instant it is released, as far as the knuckle permits. However, both methods can be used only as emergency remedies. They risk excessive tension on the base (hand and forearm); hence they could lead to severe tightness. Too few pianists realize that such tightness, which is erroneously blamed on a tightening of the wrist itself, results chiefly from faulty finger action—that is, the higher and more rounded the finger action, the more the long tendons that pass under and over the wrist bind the wrist as if it were in a vise. Moreover, with a wrist tightly bound there is no "universal joint" by which the arm can adapt to bumps in its "road"—that is, the ups and downs of black- and white-key positions and of short and long fingers.

As it happens, high finger raising still survives as the standard mode of playing among many pianists, a mode that stems from Czerny and his contemporaries. In a valuable study called *The Riddle of the Pianist's Finger* (listed under Source References), Arnold Schultz concludes largely in favor of a flatter finger that is best worked primarily by the small muscles (lumbricales) of the hand—that is, by the muscles that connect the finger's first phalanx to the palm or underside of the hand rather than the forearm muscles and their connecting tendons, which may be seen and felt both on the topside of the hand and the underside of the wrist.

The forearm muscles and their tendons excel only in force and in the higher finger raising, the latter being helpful especially in rapid finger staccato and in harpsichord playing. Otherwise, the small muscles do seem to offer numerous significant advantages. They avoid the long tendons that can cause the wrist binding just mentioned. They save energy not only by being smaller but also by working only on the down finger stroke, leaving the return stroke merely to the elastic pull of the web of the skin (contrary to the "antagonistic" muscles that are needed to effect both the down and up strokes of all the pianist's other levers). The small muscles also save energy by causing the finger to push forward through its two inner joints or knuckles, thereby starting right from the key surface (prepared attack) and approaching the direction of key travel most efficiently (about forty-five degrees downward and forward). In turn, starting from the key surface means more sensitive control, as will be discussed in Chapter 4 under "Touch and Tone." Obviously, it also means better legato. And just as obviously, it also means more speed (in relatively light playing) because of the saving in both energy and distance of finger travel.

When the small muscles are used, any finger raising above the keys becomes a waste of time and energy. But this fact does not mean the fingers should not be worked with conscious pressure and effort. Very popular in recent years has been the opposite idea of "dripping" the fingers effortlessly into the keys from a hand suspended loosely at the wrist and undulated by arm rotation. This fluent method, easiest for players with long slim fingers, has its values in rapid, velvety, legato, Chopinesque passages. But it is only one style of playing. It certainly does not answer for the neat articulation required in much other passagework. By all means, the use of the fingers must not become a lost art!

This same finger stroke that solves Mr. Schultz's intriguing "Riddle" ties in not only with today's growing preference for flatter fingers but with a related change—to playing more on the pads than the fingertips. Both the flatness and the pads aggravate the student's perennial problem of "breaking," or caving-in, at the finger's inner joints, especially in long, thin fingers. In fact, students seem to round their fingers deliberately to escape that problem. But here is an instance where it generally proves better to join than fight. If the student simply will allow, even encourage, the caving-in to occur with the flatter finger, the weak muscles in the finger's inner phalanges will get the needed exercise to grow stronger in good time, whereupon the finger can hold its desired shape.

Sometimes the rounded finger's more perpendicular stroke may even induce the breaking at the joints, especially if the fingernail is too long, thus causing the finger to skid into a flatter position with its tip turned up like a boat prow. This fact and the nuisance of clicking sounds are, incidentally, reasons enough why all pianists must file (never bite or cut!) their nails regularly. In any case, there are certain pianists who cannot use the perpendicular stroke because their nails cannot be trimmed above the fingertips without causing soreness.

Actually, the tightly rounded finger that was formerly prescribed is not only unnatural, it is impractical. If it follows through the circular arc that it describes, as it must if its position is to be maintained, then it tends to strike the key at an inward tangent, whereas, as we have seen, a flatter finger can achieve a more direct stroke. The tangential stroke reduces the finger's force substantially. Furthermore, a too-rounded finger reduces the stretch substantially and even constrains the hand action. To determine just how rounded his fingers should be, the student needs only to observe them, according to the time-honored advice, when his arms are hanging freely at his sides.

The thumb action obviously differs from that of the other fingers, to which it is in a sense opposed. It has a freer orbit and moves more easily sideways than up and down. If we had twenty vertical-axis fingers on a hand we could probably play them in succession as rapidly as we can play a twenty-tone glissando. But with only five fingers, one of which (the thumb) does all the shifting and another of which (the fifth) plays only the final notes, we seem to encounter a sort of supersonic barrier to unlimited speed. I say "seem" because in actuality the thumb does not have to hold back the other fingers. The reason it does so may very well be that too much is made of its special type of movement.

Take, for example, the old rule widely taught in scale playing that says the thumb must "snap" ahead, as if released from a slingshot, to the next note it will play the very instant it is succeeded by the second finger. This brisk act looks admirable when the scale is played slowly and imparts much the same sense of robust, muscular vigor that we get from doing our "daily dozen" each morning. It can even help the hand to avoid the quick hoisting of the wrist at the moment the thumb passes under, a fault that produces severe humps in the scale. Yet, curiously, the faster the scale is played the more this snap shift becomes a hindrance rather than a help. Snapping the thumb under the hand while the other fingers are in motion is not a wholly fluent act. It seems to require the previous finger to serve as a pivot. The momentary delay thus entailed stands out increasingly as the speed increases.

Note that this rule about the thumb action is applied only when the hand plays outward from the thumb side or center of the piano. Yet, again curiously, most pianists agree that the hand can play more easily, smoothly, and rapidly when it returns to the center. Why do we not apply the same rule on the return, posting the thumb ahead each time it is released? Whatever the answer, the student who is not taught to snap his thumb under his hand seldom has any trouble with it. He will probably do best if he is told merely to play the scale outward from the center as if the hand were pulled along a lateral track by the elbow, yet not so rigidly as to cut out slight compensatory play at the wrist joint. Then the thumb will trail along the edge of the keys and have no difficulty taking its place, in its proper turn, with the other fingers. Furthermore, the lead by the elbow tends to favor the forward finger stroke recommended above. The same position may be used on the return, with the elbow pushing instead of pulling.

The rapid staccato that was mentioned as a function of high finger raising comes from popping each finger back at the knuckle as it is released. It works best in elflike passages that exceed the speed, if not the endurance, possible to hand staccato from the wrist. A charming example, still familiar to many teachers, is the right-hand accompaniment throughout most of the return in Tchaikovsky's "Troïka," Op. 37, No. 11. Legato is often induced better not so much by analyzing the finger action as by asking the student to "hug" closer and closer to the keys, using less and less finger movement. As always, he will be greatly helped by first hearing and seeing what is wanted. Mr. Loesser calls attention to the "synthetic nature" of all legato on the piano:

> A true legato consists of making two or more successive tones with one impulse (bow, breath, and so on). Such a thing is impossible on a keyboard instrument, and can only be simulated.

While on the subject of legato, I should mention two other difficulties. One is the plodding or choppy effect that seems to come in certain passages in spite of the most careful finger legato. It shows up particularly in the even 8th- and 16th-note passages that are so common in music of moderate tempo by Bach. One antidote for this effect is to place slightly more emphasis on the regular rhythmic groupings, giving just that degree of nuance and sense of direction within those groupings that the character of the music permits. The nuance or, for that matter, any gradual change of volume and the clear rhythmic organization combine to give a distinct illusion of legato over and above that achieved by the fingers. A second antidote is to hold every finger down after it has played until it has to play again. This unlikely-sounding remedy works better than might be supposed, because Bach's characteristically tortuous lines allow only a minimum of holding down, anyway, yet a minimum that is enough to give the illusion of a better legato. In fact, it might be said to supply all the pedal effect that many of those lines can tolerate.

The other difficulty occurs in trying to make two successive octaves or other double-notes sound legato when one of the fingers has to be repeated. If both fingers try to play legato at once, the result is that neither one does. The remedy is to lift off the repeated finger before the other finger moves. That leaves one finger to be played legato (it is better if this can be the finger for the upper note), creating the illusion that both notes have been approached legato.

Here a word of caution is needed. Beyond choosing the most appropriate touch and any necessary variant (such as the high-finger staccato), the pianist can easily go astray in his efforts to control all the subtle gradations between staccato, semilegato (or *portato*, wrongly called *portamento*), legato, and actual overlapping. Thus, he will fail if he tries consciously and consistently to regulate the interval between the release of one key and the depression of the next. Even if the notes do not come along too thick and fast, his results will sound too studied. Rather he must do what any pianist has to do after he has gotten as far on the right track as he reasonably can with technical analysis. He must then turn more fully to the musical goals and hope that intuition will solve what problems still remain in the complex body machinery (an approach discussed further in the final chapter of this book).

The Use of the Hand

The hand, too, is a vehicle for both staccato and legato. If the reader wonders why so much importance is attached to a thorough command of staccato and legato, he must remind himself that in essence these cover everything that can be done by way of varied attack and release at the piano. The violinist can choose from an extraordinary variety of bowings (not to mention pizzicato), he can swell or diminish the tone at will, and he can qualify the tone by differing degrees of vibrato and by sensitive intonation. The pianist, on the other hand, can control but two things: the volume of the tone at the instant of attack and the duration of the tone while it lasts. That is all. On these two controls must depend everything that constitutes style and interpretation in piano music. (Of course, that is a little like saying that on yes and no alone must depend all the solutions reached by the computer. The number of dispositions of yes and no is itself beyond calculation!)

The function of the hand is the converse of the function of the fingers. The chief duty of the hand is to play staccato, but it can be a major agent in legato playing when it is flexibly combined with the finger action. Among the staccato uses for the hand are the playing of octaves and other double-notes, of chords within comfortable reach, and of all single notes, whether separate or grouped, that are not too fast for the wrist action. The essential point in playing crisp staccatos is to get off the key in a hurry as if it were a hot coal that had been touched. As a teacher once instructed me, "When you pay a short visit, what matters is not how soon you get there but how soon you leave." Anything that delays the release will spoil the crispness of the staccato. In other words, if the finger joints "break" so that the hand does not play in one piece from wrist to fingertips, or if the forearm jogs along without providing the firm, unyielding base for the wrist fulcrum, the finger will linger on the key before actually releasing it.

Depending on the context, there are two preferred means of leaving the key instantly. One is to start from above the key, drop the hand on a finger locked from knuckle to tip, and rebound from the wrist. This means is used to play a succession of staccato notes. A common fault occurs when the student timidly drops his finger to the key level and hesitates an instant to find the place—with, of course, the complete loss of rebound. Note, too, that continuous rebounding offers no mechanical advantage unless it is fast enough to be genuine rebounding. To understand that point, try slowing the rebound of a bouncing ball.

The other means of release is necessary wherever the hand must start from the keyboard rather than above, as at the end of a legato phrase or slur, thus making the rebound impossible. It is needed only for one staccato at a time, since, for any other staccatos that may follow, the hand will immediately be in position to rebound once more. To play this kind of staccato, the hand must draw back sharply at the wrist (taking care not to grow tense in mid-air); in fact, it must seem to strike the note by drawing back. Again, if the student questions the value of this much detail, he must be assured that these methods of release are among the most essential technical means for putting life and sparkle into his playing. They are indispensable, for example, to the spirited performance of most quick music by Haydn, Mozart, and Beethoven.

Successful octaves depend a great deal on the stretch and the structure of the hand. Stretch is determined as much by the width of the webs between the fingers as by the length of the fingers themselves. Pianists can often manage one kind of stretch and not another, as may be realized when attempting such differently constructed chords as those in Example 8. Of course, there are stretches in music that give trouble to almost all pianists; but the performer who cannot reach a minor tenth from a black to a white key (and cannot afford the smaller, custom-built keyboard

EXAMPLE 8

once used by Josef Hofmann) must expect to reduce the notes of the larger chords or break or roll them by starting before the beat. Players with a narrow stretch may find that the effort to reach an octave inhibits or tightens the wrist action to the point where the octaves must be played by the forearm working in one piece with the hand and fingers.

To be sure, there are always a few staunch advocates of the fore-arm method of playing octaves, anyway. But most pianists prefer to use their hands, with the forearm serving as nearly as possible as an immobile base. To get the feel of true hand action, the student may start by exaggerating the vertical movement of each hand (waving goodbye) throughout the complete range at the wrist hinge. Thereafter, he will discover that one secret of rapid, fluent octaves, as, indeed, of all advanced physical effort, is minimum motion. Any sound of key slap must be eliminated in efficient octave playing. Helpful insofar as the stretch permits are a slightly arched hand and an elevated wrist, with firm fingers working in a single unit with the hand.

Octaves on black keys are normally played with the thumb and fourth, or even third, finger so as to avoid the clumsy to-and-fro motion that the black and white keys otherwise cause and to enable chromatic octaves to be played legato. This principle presupposes that the white octaves will be played by the thumb and fifth finger as far in as the edge of the black keys. For legato playing, the fourth finger is sometimes needed on white octaves, too. The stretch from the thumb is usually about the same to the third, fourth, and fifth fingers because of their different lengths. But please note that when the pianist strains too hard to reach octaves with his third or fourth finger, the results will be exactly what he means to avoid: hardness, nonlegato, and clumsiness. For accurate leaps to black octaves, the fourth finger has the advantage of a larger, flatter undersurface than the fifth.

The Use of the Forearm, Upper Arm, and Trunk

Employed in single, one-piece units, the forearm and upper arm can perform heavy chords and octaves with that strength needed, for example, in the popular concertos by Liszt, Tchaikovsky, and Rachmaninov. The forearm, being faster and better controlled, is naturally used more often in this way than the upper arm. Only infrequently does either unit strike from the full height to which its joint (elbow or shoulder) permits it to be raised. Yet, I recall that just such a procedure was almost a mannerism with Paderewski. That rare artist, whose technique alone would not have ranked him among the world's greatest virtuosos, did have a way of raising his arm and hand high above his head so that he could crash them down in a single unit from the shoulder, striking his chord with uncanny accuracy and all the while transfixing his audience with a cold stare. In such attacks the arm must indeed remain locked in one piece, for a collapse at the wrist can only dissipate the force of the attack. (Recall the rubber-handled hoe.) Of course, tempo permitting, the wrist may yield up or down just enough to absorb the edge of the shock, like a resilient buffer. To avoid sounding and looking brittle requires some vertical give-and-take at the wrist, much as down-up violin bowing requires lateral wrist play.

The forearm and upper arm have also been mentioned as prime movers of the hand. Either mechanism can bring the hand to the attack and can withdraw it for the release. And either can move it to a new center of activity—to a new locale, as it were. This time the upper arm, having a wider and more complete range of motion, is more often used than the forearm. Sometimes the shifting from center to center of activity becomes very rapid, a lively example being the octave transpositions of the five-finger, 64th-note figure in the "Scherzo" of Beethoven's Sonata in E-flat, Op. 31, No. 3 (measures 90–93). The shifting becomes still more rapid in wide-range hand crossing between single notes. Then, at fast tempos, the upper arm (always meaning the entire arm as a one-piece, locked unit) must fall into an oscillating trajectory from the shoulder, rebounding back and forth (as in Domenico Scarlatti's virtuosic Sonata in A, L. 345, K. 113, measures 49–52).

The trunk, working in one piece from the hips to the finger pads, has a limited application, yet a special value in addition to what the four main mechanisms or levers offer. It is too large, relatively, to be used other than for single separated attacks and releases (corresponding to a low-low gear in that automotive stickshift analogy made earlier). But because of its relative size and weight, it can achieve exceptional control. For example, the trunk's use to start off a slow movement, such as the "Adagio cantabile" in Beethoven's *Grande Sonate pathétique,* is perhaps the surest means of achieving the desired quantity and balance of tone. It then helps the pianist somewhat the way the fullest breath support or bow arm helps to insure the purity and steadiness of a long, gradually swelling tone at the start of a vocal aria (as in "Pace, pace, mio Dio!" from Verdi's *La Forza del destino*) or of a violin piece (as in the "Adagio" from Bach's Concerto in E). The angle of key attack when the trunk is used from the hips is excellent, with reference to that ideal downward-forward approach of about forty-five degrees. Furthermore, when one is getting under way in public performance, the larger mechanisms seem to succumb less than the smaller ones to the physical effects of nervousness.

Some Combination Touches

As for the various combination touches, their misuses must be known in order to profit from their good uses. We have already seen how control diminishes as the number of touch mechanisms increases. We have also seen how the arm can hamper hand or finger action by jogging along and not providing a firm base against which these lighter levers can react. And there are those excessive arm rotations that show up mostly in slow, expressive playing, including undulating wrists and elbows like wing tips! Their doubtful use to "free" the arm or stimulate rhythmic flow is surely canceled by their mechanical disadvantages as well as their distracting, sentimental appearance to the audience. Of course, no rotary motion is likely to succeed if the posture is slumped. Then, as suggested earlier, the shoulders are bound and their use is even overlooked.

But with these hazards duly recalled and disposed of in advance, it is important to realize how valuable the upper arm in particular can be as a prime agent in combination touches. Its main function in this capacity is to serve as the impetus for a series of two or more notes played by the hand or fingers. At the same time it provides a source of additional strength and endurance. Thus, in an extended passage of octaves in either or both hands, the upper arm can give a helpful impetus to each rhythmic group of whatever number of octaves (usually three or four). To get the feel of that procedure, which dates back at least to Chopin's time, the student might first practice each group in place, as in Example 9.

The upper arm gives its impetus on the first of each group by dropping vertically from the shoulder through the wrist hinge

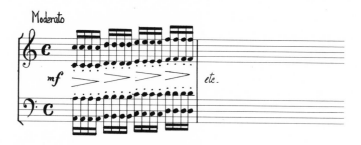

EXAMPLE 9

(somewhat the way the violinist's arm shifts horizontally from the shoulder through the wrist at each change of bow). Then the hand and wrist can play the remaining octaves of the group as diminishing (almost) free rebounds, like the several rebounds of a rubber ball after it is thrown to the ground. At the same time, the hand and wrist gradually rise through the rebounds so as to be in position for the next impetus or arm drop from the shoulder. Timing that rise and then the drop on the first of each new group without any break in the rhythm is part of the technique to be mastered. Remember that genuine rebounds cannot occur below a certain speed, so that this technique needs to occur at tempos that are at least moderate. That the problem of endurance can be helped greatly by the impetus from the upper arm will quickly be realized by any pianist who has tried to survive unscathed without it through the pages of octaves in Liszt's *Hungarian Rhapsody* No. 6 or the "accompaniment" of Schubert's "Erlking."

Extreme illustrations of the same technique occur when there are veritable cascades of octaves, as in Example 10, from Chopin's Fantasy in F minor. In effect, one must use one broad golf stroke (for each staff) to hit a whole series of golf balls arranged on progressively higher tees. Here is one of the countless instances, it might be added, where the problem is to find the *athletically most*

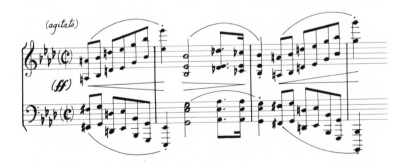

EXAMPLE 10

graceful solution. And that solution, as here, is most often a *curve of force* initiated by the upper arm. When the pianist sees the truth of this idea he literally gets the "swing" of it.

The upper arm can also supply the impetus for finger passages. Another fine example from Chopin is the opening of the "Revolutionary" Etude, where the accent on the start of each group of four 16th-notes can be achieved only by that means (Example 11).

EXAMPLE 11

The fingers have neither the strength nor the time at that speed suddenly to strike conspicuously harder. On the upper arm's help depends many a rocketing passage like that one (or the rising passage in both hands that occurs twice in the first movement of Beethoven's Sonata in C minor, Op. 111, measures 67–69 and 144–146). As with the octaves, the arm impetus is a drop from the shoulder through the wrist. The drop is easier to manage when it can occur on an outer finger (as noted later under fingering), mainly because a slight turn out or in of the entire locked arm seems to secure this technique.

The impetus from the upper arm is essential, too, in the two-note slur, especially in the series of two-note slurs that were so common in the late eighteenth and early nineteenth centuries. Example 12, from Mozart's Sonata in F, K. 533 and 494, is representative. Because the upper arm has so little time to recover (only one note),

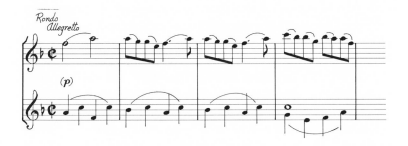

EXAMPLE 12

its action must be minimal. In fact, the observer can scarcely detect this action if the pianist's arm is covered by a full-length sleeve. Yet, it takes only minimal action of the larger, more remote levers to achieve the necessary results. (Imagine what little action would be required in your upper arm even to write your name on a blackboard in letters two feet high provided you used a locked arm extended by a ten-foot pole with a piece of chalk at the end!) To get the swing of this technique, the student can try going up and down his scales in two-note slurs (by repeating each note), hands together, using each pair of fingers in turn. As the speed increases and the arm action becomes minimal, he must take care that that action does not stop altogether. His way of checking, and his teacher's, too, will be to make sure that each two-note slur continues to go from strong to weak dynamically. If the accent starts shifting to each second note, then he knows the technique has gone awry.

A very few techniques depend on combination touches that involve all four main mechanisms in a kind of chain reaction. One is rapid repeated notes, which set up a spiral motion in the arm from shoulder to fingertips (not pads). The fingers sweep the key as if they were the bristles on a rotary brush turning toward the back of the key, in the order 3–2–1 or 4–3–2–1 (not the reverse). The upper arm and forearm help to reposition the hand and fingers for each sweep so that there is no audible interruption. Another such technique is "rotary motion," so called, which too often is prescribed as a kind of vitamin C for all piano-playing ailments, but which does have clear values within narrower limits. Rotary motion that passes through the entire arm helps to compensate for the short thumb and fifth finger. It succeeds best when the figure spans at least a sixth, when the tempo is moderate or faster, and when the passage actually rotates (as is true especially in the left hand at the start of Chopin's "Aeolian Harp" Etude but not in the right hand at the end of his *Fantaisie Impromptu*). When the figure is slower and more minutely expressive, as at the start of Beethoven's "Moonlight" Sonata, the fingers alone provide much surer control.

The forearm combines with the fingers by oscillating at the radio-ulnar joint to play a tremolo. This technique tends to fail when the stretch is less than a sixth, becoming impossible as the sole means of trilling adjacent keys in spite of frequent teaching to the contrary. And it tends to fail when the volume grows too great, causing the forearm to lock in with the full arm in a motion too wild to control.

Finally among combination touches, the hand may work in conjunction with, but independently of, the fingers to produce a very pliant legato and secure grasp of the keys. To achieve this technique, the student must learn to move the fingers and hand laterally at the knuckles and wrist at least as much as he moves them vertically. The process is an art in itself and one that affords the pianist a pleasurable and confident sense of being in control. The process is also one that is easier seen and felt than described, because it seems to come from within the hand. The pianist must think of fitting right into the varied molds formed by the myriad positions among the black and white keys. He must feel that he is reaching forward and to either side, in a most flexible, supple manner, to play whatever lies within range without budging the forearm. (Among possible analogies for the student are the kneading of dough for baking bread, the working with modeling clay, or the walking of a big, slow spider.) This approach to the keyboard is especially appropriate in Bach's music when it becomes necessary for one hand to maintain the contrapuntal integrity of two or more expressive, legato lines.

3. More Technique:
The Basic Exercises

WE ARE REPEATEDLY REMINDED, though rarely with concrete remedies, that we tend to regard technique as an end in itself instead of a means to musical ends. I remember calling on a prominent cellist whose main advice was that "technique is everything. What you must have, my boy, is technique, *more* technique, and *more* technique!" I also seem to remember a cellist in a Dickens novel who practiced scales all day long and did so because he found his satisfaction in the exercise itself. Most of us, however, really mean to be in the field of music for music's sake. The big question, then, is whether we are taking the right means to achieve this end.

Do Formal Studies Serve Their Purpose?

The conviction has grown in recent years among many teachers and performers that pianists often go overboard in the use of exercises. They glorify the exercise to the point where it is done as a matter of course and for its own sake, quite apart from the goal it should implement. Not that anyone questions a basic need for *some* exercises and drills. The question is simply this: Are we choosing exercises that will meet that need or are we merely doing any and all exercises on the treacherous assumption that somehow, somewhere, whatever we do will apply?

It is hard to think of another field in which a complete formal program of extracurricular conditioning is maintained similarly alongside the main study. One frequently hears it said, though not in the field of music, that each person gets enough exercise for his chosen pursuit directly from the activities inherent in the pursuit itself. This idea applies equally to mental and physical activities. The typist keeps up and improves her typing primarily by typing the daily work allotted to her; the errand boy builds up his necessary stamina simply by running his daily errands; the certified public accountant keeps in trim by figuring his daily accounts. To be sure, dancers, athletes, and others who specialize in physical skills do use warm-up exercises. But even these people train themselves more and more by reproducing as nearly as possible the circumstances of the contests they will be entering.

Even in the early stages of these pursuits, it is doubtful that the beginner does better, if as well, to train on abstract exercises rather than problems that grow out of his actual experience. It is doubtful, for example, that the typist who drills by the hour on "Now is the time for all good men . . ." learns to type as soon as the one who starts in with the newer drills based on real-life correspondence and manuscripts. Yet the host of pianists, by and large, stick faithfully to their formal program of Czerny's *Art of Finger Dexterity,* Clementi's *Gradus ad Parnassum*, Cramer's *Selected Studies,* Hanon's *Daily Exercises,* and Pischna's *Finger Studies,* enjoying the exhilaration of the ascetic who contemplates the finer things that lie beyond.

For most of Pischna, Hanon, and the like, there is really little excuse. Only a kind of psychological lethargy can account for the loyalty to their monotonous compilations. The teacher has almost no explaining to do, the student has very little note reading to worry him, and the mind is free to wander into subjects far removed while the required practice minutes tick by. No harm is done, no tempers are ruffled, and—alas!—little or no good is accomplished. For Czerny, Clementi, Cramer, and their contemporaries there may be more justification, if only because much of their music has charm and some of it depth.

The vital point, however, is that the practice of a Czerny study leads mainly to the perfection of that Czerny study rather than to Beethoven or Chopin or composers in general. The way to learn Beethoven is to practice Beethoven. The practice of Czerny can help Beethoven only when the same passage happens to occur in both, and such practice can mean wasting a lot of valuable time. The psychologists will corroborate this statement with, "Why, of course that's so; you musicians are slow to make that discovery. We reached that conclusion when we generally discarded the old theory of transfer of training." The old theory said that mathematics and chess were food for the brain, but now we know that the study of these only makes mathematicians and chess players. We still hear that Latin is a valuable course because it helps with English grammar. There *are* basic principles in Latin that do carry over, but if those were the only reasons for studying Latin, how much easier it would be just to study in English the roots, construction, and syntax that apply.

The main fallacy in adhering to Czerny *et al.* lies, it seems to me, in the illusion that piano practice means the development of the piano-playing muscles in general. But it does not. It means developing specific muscular coordinations to meet specific situations. There are woodsmen and athletes who can squeeze any pianist's hand to a pulp. But their splendid strength means nothing at the piano, for unless they have practiced the act they can barely set down five fingers in a row. One learns only what one practices. Each technical feat must be learned separately. Technique does not generalize. The most that can happen in general is that the pianist will acquire enough specific experiences to enable him to meet almost whatever confronts him. This idea would suggest that Czerny can at least supply the pianist with further experiences, though, here again, common sense dictates that if our main interest lies in performing other music, the other music is where we should seek those experiences.

Now, having stated my case against the regular use of studies for the sake of exercise, I hasten to add this brief but important qualification: There are indeed times when a certain study will answer a special need very well. A study may be found that counteracts a peculiar mannerism or strengthens a conspicuous weakness. (In fact, to meet such needs is the reason most of the well-known studies were written.) Then the particular study does merit practice, but only as needed and not on general principle. (This conclusion is reached notwithstanding the well-known report that when Paderewski went to Leschetizky he was put on nothing but Czerny for a year.) Meanwhile, the student must remember that there are other, usually more efficient, ways of meeting actual technical requirements.

Making the Most of Scales and Other Drills

Many teachers have come to feel that the careful practice of certain basic drills will suffice for all warm-up and extracurricular technical requirements. Some have invented their own drill sequences, as elaborate and useless as Hanon can be. Others have singled out the standard drills of all pianists, five of which are indeed basic: trills, scales, arpeggios, octaves, and double-notes. Exercises that are based on these five types of drills and that are practiced in standard rhythms immediately have one argument in their favor. Their basic figures do repeatedly occur, exactly as they may be practiced, in a great deal of piano music written from the early 1600s to the late 1800s. These figures are less likely to occur, say, in Hindemith, Bartók, or Milhaud and become less and less applicable in contemporary music.

Liszt and Paderewski are two among a number of the world's great pianists who reportedly concluded that the simple trill is the fundamental piano exercise. A helpful and quick way to practice the trill is as follows: With the hands playing together, place the thumbs on g and c'. Begin the trill of the first and second fingers slowly, in triplet rhythm (so that each finger gets the exercise value of the accents), as in Example 13. Gradually in-

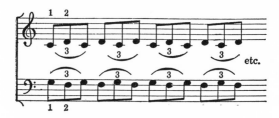

EXAMPLE 13

crease the speed locomotive style, dropping the triplet rhythm when it gets too fast to manage, until the maximum even speed is attained. Continue trilling as smoothly as possible until the palms seem to tire, which may be less than a minute if the small hand muscles operate the fingers, as recommended in the previous chapter. The remaining fingers may be exercised similarly, in contrary motion, in the order 4–5, 2–3, and 3–4, so as to give them the best chance to rest between trills.

The further trill positions that result from doing the same drill a half step higher each time are useful, too. Moreover, each group of three fingers—1–2–3, 3–4–5, 2–3–4—may be exercised in a similar manner, equally applicable to many musical situations. This last drill may start as in Example 14.

After the rudiments of scales and arpeggios have been shown

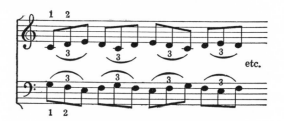

EXAMPLE 14

to him in C major, the student should learn these drills in all the keys, major and minor, all at the same time. Even beginners seem to progress more rapidly and more securely with this perspective of the whole, based on over-all principles of fingering, than if they master each key before progressing to the next. However, since there is not time to do all of them each day, the keys should be rotated throughout the circle over fairly brief periods of time. For example, the following schedule fills one six-day week at the rate of two major and two tonic (rather than relative) minor keys per day:

DAILY KEY CHART

Mon.	C—c	F♯(G♭)—f♯
Tues.	G—g	D♭(C♯)—c♯
Wed.	D—d	A♭—a♭(g♯)
Thurs.	A—a	E♭—e♭(d♯)
Fri.	E—e	B♭—b♭(a♯)
Sat.	B(C♭)—b	F—f

The student might conveniently follow the same schedule for his other drill exercises and his playing by ear.

Here, then, are some over-all principles of fingering that should obviate individual scale fingerings. Since all major and minor scale forms contain seven notes in each "octave," and since the hand can only take in seven notes by alternating three plus four fingers (not five plus two), the main problem is where in those seven notes to start that alternation of three plus four. In other words, which two notes will the thumb fall on? The answer is best given for the outward direction of the scale (right hand to the right and left to the left). Then these two rules and their few exceptions will cover all situations: (1) Finger all major and minor scales with white tonics in the order 1–2–3 1–2–3–4 except those on F in the right hand and B in the left, which obviously have to be 1–2–3–4 1–2–3 to avoid the thumb on a black key. (2) Still thinking outward from the center, start all major and minor scales with black tonics on the second finger and put the thumb on the first white key (obvious exceptions: B-flat and E-flat harmonic minor in the left hand) as well as on the white key following the further black key(s).

The second finger is traditionally preferred to start on black tonics because it requires the least stretch when the hand rounds the inner corner of the scale, even though the third or fourth finger will come out on the succeeding black tonics in certain of the scales. To finger all scales in the opposite direction, right hand to the left and left hand to the right, simply use the same fingering in reverse (except for obvious changes when the right hand descends on F-sharp and C-sharp melodic minor). Alternative scale fingerings have been proposed from time to time, much as alternative layouts of the keyboard itself have been proposed (see "Keyboard" in the *Harvard Dictionary of Music*). Mainly, they are designed to utilize the thumb on black keys (as is done with good effect in many other situations) and to improve scale playing in parallel octaves by making the groups of threes and fours coincide in the two hands. But thus far the disadvantages to learning, fluent speed, and legato have seemed at least to equal the advantages.

The chief fingering problem that arpeggios raise lies in the choice between the third or fourth finger, since the other three fingers—one, two, and five—nearly always take part anyway. There are justifiable disagreements on this choice, based on differences in relative finger lengths from one player to the next (or between the man and the woman pianist if the difference noted earlier holds true). These disagreements arise mainly in first-inversion chords. However, the most usual choice in all four-note chords that cover an octave or more is the fourth finger when the two tones farthest from the thumb are two white or two black keys not more than a major third apart or any two keys not more than a minor third apart. Otherwise, the choice is the third finger.

Sample uses of the third and the fourth fingers appear in Example 15.

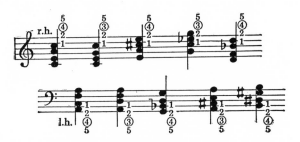

EXAMPLE 15

With reference again to the outward direction—the right hand arpeggiating to the right or the left hand to the left—the thumb starts each of the three positions in chords with white keys only or black keys only, and it frequently is preferred for starting even the two black-key positions in chords with only one white key. But it is not usually used for starting the only black-key position in chords with two white keys. Instead, the fingering for either of the white-key positions becomes the basis for that of the black-key position. Thus, in the D major triad, the second position, with the right hand ascending from F-sharp, may be fingered 2–3–1–2 or 4–1–2–4, as in Example 16; but, for the sake of uniformity, it

EXAMPLE 16

seems preferable and just as easy always to use the fingering of the position that begins on the lowest white key in the triad, which would be 2–3–1–2 in the example cited. Further applications of this principle are shown in Example 17. (But, as in black-tonic scales, the second finger commonly would start the outward motion in such black-key positions in order to ease the turning of the inner corner regardless of the subsequent fingering.)

EXAMPLE 17

Besides certain faults in the finger, hand, and arm action that are to be discussed, unsure fingering and failure to cover the notes properly often explain weak scales and arpeggios. In other words, the weakness is at least as likely to be mental as physical, meaning an *inability to think through the notes fast enough* rather than any mechanical sluggishness. An intelligent corrective is supplied

EXAMPLE 18

by playing these exercises in simultaneous blocks of notes, or "clusters," according to the grouping of the fingers. From a learning standpoint, this is again like conceiving groups of letters as syllables. In Example 18 the clusters for the D major and E-flat harmonic minor scales are shown as fingered for both the left and right hands. Similarly, the clusters for the three positions of the E major arpeggio are shown in Example 19. A feeling for the

EXAMPLE 19

shape or mold of the cluster can be induced either by playing the clusters (1) staccato with hand action from the wrist and no give in the fingers (as in the playing of octaves) or (2) legato, isolating the thumb so that it alternates with the remaining block of fingers in each cluster, as in Example 20.

EXAMPLE 20

Each hand should be mastered separately, after which the clusters may be tried hands together. The student should at least be able to cover the scale range (two octaves, or whatever) faster with clusters than with individual finger action. When he sees how and why the scale clusters do not coincide in the two hands, he will be able to cope better with that conflicting fingering that results from playing the scales in parallel motion. Occasionally he should return to the clusters to renew their feel. This feel is also developed, as in sight-reading, by trying never to look at the keyboard, even during arpeggios! For proof recall the secure grasp of the keys ("position technique") by most blind pianists.

Here, too, are some general principles for fingering scales in thirds. The problem now becomes how to allocate three plus four *pairs* of fingers to seven double-notes. There is fairly wide agreement on the C major scale, which may be played as in Example 21. The solution is three pairs of fingers plus two times two

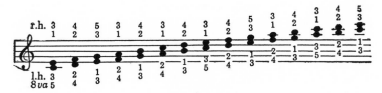

EXAMPLE 21

pairs. However, a variety of fingerings has been advocated for all the other scales with one or more sharps or flats. It is my belief that the simplicity of using one fingering for all major and natural minor keys outweighs the small advantages to be gained by learning many different fingerings. The seven double-notes in the octave may invariably be fingered $\frac{3-4-5}{1-2-3}$ $\frac{2-3-4-5}{1-1-2-3}$ in the outward direction, the one question being at what point in that fingering series to start each scale. As a help, the student should remember that, for either hand, scales with white tonics begin with the thumb on the tonic; those with black tonics begin so that the thumb will fall on a white key at the beginning of both the $\frac{3-4-5}{1-2-3}$ and the $\frac{2-3-4-5}{1-1-2-3}$ groups. Thus, the D major and E-flat natural minor scales will be played as in Example 22.

Fingerings may also be recommended here for certain other double-note scales that give trouble. In Example 23 the chromatic scale in minor thirds is fingered so as to take advantage of the slide from a black to a white key. It will be noted that the slide

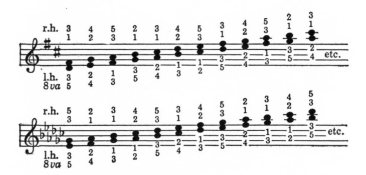

EXAMPLE 22

occurs only on the second finger and only from a black key that precedes two white keys. The scales in sixths may be fingered similarly to those in thirds, with $\frac{4-5}{2-3}$ always becoming $\frac{4-5}{1-2}$. The chromatic scale in major sixths may be played without slides, as in Example 24, by those who can manage the stretches. An alternative is to eliminate the fifth finger by substituting 1–3 for each 2–5, sliding on the thumb each time and also sliding (or attempting to slide) on 4 wherever it can avoid 3 twice in succession.

There are various other drills that are useful, too, because they apply directly in much music. For example, there are trills in thirds, $\frac{3-4}{1-2}$ and $\frac{4-5}{2-3}$, which may be practiced according to the pattern of Example 13. (I shall never forget the remarkably fine recital of a pianist resourceful, agile, and artistic enough to build it

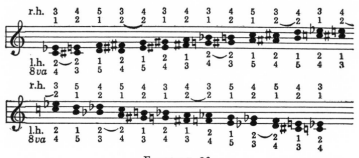

EXAMPLE 23

EXAMPLE 24

entirely from pieces in double-notes, which he had come to view, with good reason, as a panacea for nearly all technical ills.) There is the chromatic scale, which may be fingered according to the traditional method, in the outward direction, of 1–3 from a white to a black key and 1–2–3 when there are two white keys before the black key; or according to the method that puts the thumb on every other white key (so that the right hand going to the right from C will play 1–2–3–4 1–2–3 1–2–3–4, and so on). And there are the arpeggios on at least the white-key positions of each diminished- and dominant-seventh chord. Practicing such drills in rhythms, especially threes and fours, brings them closer to actual music applications, helps to smooth out hitches, and keeps the hands more exactly together.

Always good is the familiar instruction to set the metronome at a moderate tempo (60–80) and play a scale one octave one note to a beat once, two octaves two notes to a beat twice, and so on, adding notes to the beat even after the extreme range is reached. Scales are often brought under better control by playing them in fives, sixes (a pair of triplets), sevens (every tonic accented), and eights (a pair of fours). Frequently I have recommended experiments with extreme speeds to my students as a means of eliminating waste motion. These are the speeds they are asked to try for:

Scales: 7 notes to a beat of 120, 5 or 6 octaves
Arpeggios: 12 notes to a beat of 60, 4 octaves
Octave scales: 4 notes to a beat of 116, 3 or 4 octaves

These speeds may seem out of the question at first. But most students can approximate them as they learn to cut out superfluous tension, unnecessary finger raising, pounding, and other excesses to be discussed presently. Naturally, such skimming along the keys must be counterbalanced by at least as much practice that is slower and more calculated.

Students who seek still more challenging workouts, as many do, will enjoy devising their own exercises based on the same standard drills we have been discussing. In fact, it is possible to kill not the usual two but three birds with one stone by also getting in some needed drilling in the four playing mechanisms that were discussed in the previous chapter and in the keyboard harmony discussed in the first chapter. By way of illustration, there follow eleven sample exercises (most of which appeared originally, though sometimes differently, in the *Piano Quarterly* No. 50). These are intended only as possible models for those countless similarly purposed exercises that resourceful students can readily devise for themselves. Prefacing each exercise are comments on methods and values that necessarily overlap some of our other discussions here and there. There is value, of course, in an exercise that poses a finite, tangible goal in itself, whether the problem is simply to work to the ends of the piano and back, or to work more circuitously through all the keys before returning to the starting key of C. Much of the time there is also the related problem of endurance and the need to husband the strength until the goal is reached. Examples 25 through 28 develop octave techniques and Examples 29 through 31 arpeggio techniques, both of which are too often neglected in teaching yet constantly needed in standard piano literature. Examples 32 through 35 develop scale techniques.

If such exercises seem to take us precariously close to the Hanon exercises that were rejected earlier as being dry and inefficient, it should only be necessary to re-emphasize three main differences. First, the kinds of exercises proposed here stick to those drill figures that have the most direct applications in actual music.

Second, the exercises that involve independent finger work employ rhythmic groupings that keep the accents shifting. And third, these exercises are offered not as an abstract, universal training program but only as samples of specifics to be devised by the student himself to meet whatever needs may arise.

In Example 25 the hands play staccato octaves on the white keys from the center of the keyboard (the dissonant E–F) to the ends and back. The contrary motion not only suits the natural opposition of the two arms and hands but it also discourages tendencies to look at the keys or to shift the trunk, to the left or right, with the arms. Overcoming one problem at a time, the student can first play the notes without looking, whereby his main keyboard harmony experience will be hearing when to turn back at the extremes of the keyboard. Then he can add the staccato hand motion from the wrist, the accenting in groups of four 16th-notes (complicating the turn back on an unaccented note), the counting in three-four meter, the initiation of each 16th-note group with an arm drop from the shoulders (as was advocated under combination touches), and increased speed each time with less motion. To get to the ends and back even once unscathed (without playing "in the cracks") and with all these problems under control is not easy.

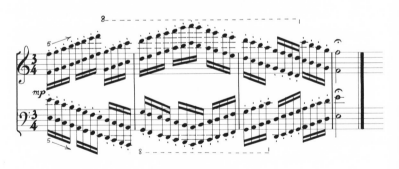

EXAMPLE 25

In Example 26 the hands again play staccato octaves in contrary motion, but this time they move chromatically within a smaller

EXAMPLE 26

total range and start on C–E so that the paths of the two hands through the white and black keys are identical (in a mirror relationship). Do not overlook the advantages and experience of putting the fourth or the third finger on black octaves and the fourth occasionally on white octaves. The step-by-step approach in Example 25 applies here, too, except that the arm drop works less well when it comes on a black octave.

Example 27 presents one of many possible modulatory patterns for going through the major (or minor) scales in octaves. Both up and down, simply play two octaves plus another step *in that scale* plus a half-step. To reach the scale of C again without undue tiring (after ten rises and falls), use minimal motion and try again

EXAMPLE 27

to initiate the first of each group of four 16th-notes with an arm drop so that the remaining three can be free rebounds. Avoid leaning to the left or right now that the arms are moving in parallel motion. To avoid interruptions, look ahead to each new change of key.

Example 28, which presents arpeggio positions in octaves, ascends through three triads, descends a half-step higher, and so on, until C is reached again. The mixing of leaps of thirds and fourths increases the problem of accuracy, especially on the triads

EXAMPLE 28

with white keys only, where no fourth finger on black octaves occurs to help focus the aim.

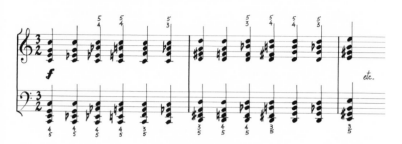

EXAMPLE 29

Example 29 merely prepares the harmonic sequence itself of both of the arpeggio exercises that it precedes. It arrives at all the white-key positions of every major and minor triad. More specifically, it arrives at six possible positions on each white key by using that key first as the root of a major and a minor triad, then as the third, and then as the fifth. To get the physical feel of these chords, let the fingers form the mold of each in the air before they are propelled by the forearm (from the elbow) in an unprepared attack (starting from above the key surface).

Example 30 indicates how each chord position in the harmonic

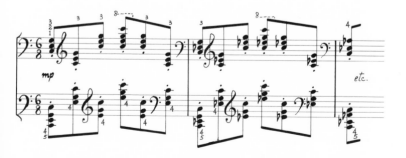

EXAMPLE 30

sequence of Example 29 may be expanded into the simultaneous clusters of a four-octave arpeggio (with the thumbs meeting at the unison only because of these clusters). One gets an insight into arpeggios at high speeds by taking all four clusters in either direction with one circular sweep of the entire arm from the shoulder (to repeat an analogy in Chapter 2, somewhat as if hitting four balls on four successive tees in one golf stroke).

EXAMPLE 31

Example 31 goes through the arpeggios themselves according to the harmonic sequence introduced in Example 29. Playing them in groups of four (rather than three) 16th-notes keeps the accent shifting from one finger to the next. Try practicing without looking at the hands or keys, which is difficult but develops a secure sense of covering the clusters. Again, avoid shifting the trunk to the right or left along with the arms, thus spoiling the aim. Yet round the corners at each end with a full-toned accent on the bottom and top. Also, try playing in one direction at a time with one parallel sweep of the arms, as if laying out the clusters of Example 30 in one continuous, steady flow of notes.

Example 32 (like Example 29) merely prepares the harmonic sequence of both of the exercises that it precedes, this time crushing the stepwise five-finger positions to be used in Examples 33 and 34—major, minor, diminished, and whole-tone—into dis-

EXAMPLE 32

sonant clusters. With four clusters on each of the twelve possible half-steps, there are forty-eight of these clusters in all. Again, use unprepared forearm attacks, shaping the mold of each cluster in the air before it is struck.

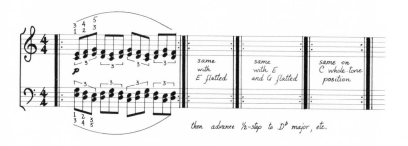

EXAMPLE 33

Example 33 provides an essential double-note drill within the clusters introduced in Example 32. The triplets keep shifting the accent to a different pair of fingers. Genuinely independent finger action is required to achieve legato in each strand of the thirds. Thirds can also help to master the flatter fingers, the playing on the pads instead of the tips, the constant contact with the key surfaces (prepared attacks), and the sense of pushing the fingers through their inner joints, techniques that were generally advocated in the previous chapter.

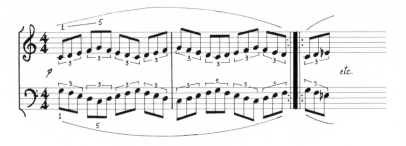

EXAMPLE 34

With Example 34 we apply the five-finger clusters of Example 32 as single notes in triplets. The thirds in Example 33 have introduced the style of relatively flat-finger action that can yield high speeds, effective legato, and sensitive control in Example 34. As the speed increases beyond the ability to accent the triplets, so the problem increases of getting the dependent fourth finger to sound. This problem is helped by a slight but accurately timed thrust of the arms outward from the shoulders just as each fifth finger rounds each outside corner.

Finally, Example 35 illustrates one of the many formulas for one continuous tour of all the major scales in octaves, sixths, and tenths, arriving back at C. Note how the change is made from octaves to sixths in the second beat of the third measure and from sixths to tenths in the last two beats of the fifth measure; note also how some fingering adjustment must be made to start each new key (as at the start of the eighth measure). For the full dose, the student can add the parallel minor scales in octaves, sixths, and tenths before advancing to each new major key a half-step higher. The shifting accents of the two triplets in each sextolet help to assure rhythmic control in actual music. (Recall the other rhythmic groupings that were recommended earlier in this chapter for scale practice.)

EXAMPLE 35

Creating Exercises out of Actual Situations

As has been stressed more than once, the chief value of all the drills discussed thus far in this chapter is that they apply directly in much standard piano literature. However, it is possible to arrive at drills that apply still more directly and in *any* piano literature. In fact, one might go so far as to say that the pianist who is resourceful, intelligent, and thorough enough in arriving at such drills will never need to bother with other kinds of exercises. The drills I have in mind are the shorter, more local sort that one creates out of actual musical situations as problems arise. The student is rare who can do such creating to the ideal degree, but the fact remains that most teachers and students fail to exploit its possibilities adequately. Shining evidence of both its efficiency and

its effectiveness has come to me in numerous instances when students have gone at pieces presumably well beyond their technical levels and then surprised me by rising to the occasion.

For example, a young lady begged to be allowed to study the now too-familiar Chopin Polonaise in A-flat major. Although this work, along with Debussy's *Clair de lune* and Lecuona's *Malagueña,* had been suffering inordinate exposure, and although she seemed to be much better prepared for the easier Chopin nocturnes, the project was approved because the factor of interest is so vital to learning. The results were astonishing and enlightening in more ways than one. Not only did they confirm what a powerful motivation interest can be and, incidentally, how effectively the old "play like me" instruction can operate (she had immediately purchased the Rubinstein recording). They also showed that careful, intelligent practice in the music itself, and in it alone, could produce specific achievements far in advance of her general technical level, thanks largely to her knack for creating self-corrective exercises out of the various difficulties that arose.

Because the technical situations vary in the extreme from one piece to the next, only a few general procedures for creating exercises can be suggested here. (On pages 189–190 are illustrated ways to convert figures or "handfuls" of notes into double-note exercises, along with specific examples.) As a prerequisite, the student should be encouraged to analyze his own difficulties as soon as he is interested in solving them. If an ascending scale in the left hand trips up his fourth finger, (1) what is wrong with the muscular action or angle of approach, and (2) what will correct it? This attitude is not only desirable but is sometimes imperative. Quirks, jerks, hitches, and skips have a way of marring a passage in spite of the most dogged practice if no effort is made to discover the cause. Try as he will, the conscientious teacher, who has advised with every general principle that comes to mind, may find that *he* cannot get at the trouble. The passage plays smoothly enough for him. The cause, for example, might lie in the hand construction or the reflexes of the student, who will then have to discover the difficulty for himself, from the inside, so to speak.

To be sure, the teacher may be able to draw upon his own experience and recognize the impediment as, for instance, a failure to cover the whole cluster or handful in which it occurs ("position technique" again), or as the consequence of a disadvantageous angle of attack, or even as nothing more than a thought hesitation that will soon be bridged over in the normal learning process.

When the student's or teacher's analysis will not solve the hitch or other difficulty, then it becomes necessary for the student to create his own exercise out of this difficulty. In so doing he must *include just enough of its context* to be sure that any improvements can be incorporated into the performance without further difficulties. Again, from Mr. Loesser:

> Eminently so. In fact, the very beginning of the troublesome passage may be compromised by a disadvantageous hand position necessitated by the previous passage. But smoothing a dubious passage into its context also helps remove the psychological tenderness created by lifting the passage out in the first place.

Out of his problem segment, the student should try to invent, with the least possible alteration, a sort of perpetual-motion figure that will strengthen or correct the weak or faulty coordination. Very often this figure will be a rotary passage that reverses its direction, after moving forward, in order to start over again without a break. For instance, the troublesome right-hand thirds at the opening of Beethoven's Sonata in C, Op. 2, No. 3, may be "exercised" as in Example 36.

EXAMPLE 36

Further help is gained, especially when one of the notes tends to be slurred over or skipped without sounding, by practicing the derived exercise in rhythms different from the source. Most commonly, triplets will be played in twos or vice versa. In this way, fingers falling on weak beats will get the exercise benefit of the changed accent. Also, the principle of playing groups of notes in simultaneous clusters can have the same comprehension value that was noted above for scales and arpeggios. For instance, the bass in measures 15 and 16 of Chopin's "Revolutionary" Etude may be practiced as in Example 37. In such treatments, the fingering of the clusters should correspond as nearly as possible to that chosen for the original passage.

EXAMPLE 37

4. Practice

IT HAS ALWAYS seemed to me that, beyond the training in fine piano music, the guiding of the practice toward the day when the student can become his own teacher is the most important mission of the piano teacher. Working himself out of a job, as it were, the teacher should help the student meet his pianistic challenges

until eventually the student makes himself independent of formal teaching. Nor should the "eventually" go on too long. Just as some grown children can never quite free themselves of their emotional dependence on their parents, so some grown students can never quite trust themselves to forge ahead without instruction. If they leave one teacher, they must move on to another. (A more aggravated form of this anomaly is the student who insists that he must continue lessons in order to be made to practice, whether out of respect for the financial investment or fear of the teacher's displeasure.) The best thing in the world for such students, who are often very advanced in their skills and experience, is the working up and presentation of a recital entirely on their own, come what may.

Now, all this is not to belittle the absolute necessity of the teacher in the training of the pianist; nor to underestimate the time this training takes, or the need for meticulous supervision, or even the value of outside criticism throughout one's musical career. The purpose here is to suggest a basic line of procedure in our teaching: help the student to help himself. Certainly, like the parent with the child, the teacher himself can be responsible for the student's dependence. He can, for example, write in the student's fingering, demonstrate his rhythms (only too often teaching them by rote), or dictate his own interpretation, until it is he and not the student who learns the piece! The student who is placed more on his own will err and he will show bad taste, of course. But he will be learning in the best way, by experience. And it is in furthering that experience that the teacher should figure. From the very start, the teacher should be the good counselor who questions the fingering, or the rhythm, or the interpretation that the student brings in, and who suggests the further possibilities from which the student chooses.

Only in this way will the student develop the creative imagination, the self-criticism, and the confidence that he must have when he is ready to carry on alone. And only in this way will the student become a complete musical personality in his own right, with the courage and independent judgment to give full expression to his own musical feelings. Indeed, only in this way will he develop the wholehearted interest that is a *sine qua non* of effective learning. (Naturally, this laissez-faire policy must not be construed as an excuse for the unimaginative teacher who merely listens in blank silence, concluding the lesson with comments that are neither constructive nor specific, such as, "Not so good; try harder next time." That sort of teacher may play well but he has not learned to teach.)

We have a first clue, now, as to how the student should practice. He must expect to lead himself with the teacher's guidance but *not be led by the hand*. Next comes the very important question, What should he practice? For a preliminary answer, we may recall the basic principle introduced with the discussion of technique: The student should practice exactly what he wants to learn and—if the practice is to attain maximum efficiency—*only* what he wants to learn. Put differently, he should examine his goal and concentrate in his practice on surmounting those obstacles that keep him from it.

This principle is one of those apparent truisms that come home with increasing force as more and more of their ramifications are appreciated. The student wants to learn to play the piano. To do this he must learn one piece after another until he has acquired the wealth of experiences that makes the well-rounded performer. From the practice standpoint, his main concern is how to go about learning a new piece. In Chapter 6, nine steps in that process are demonstrated in some detail. Here are discussed some basics that implement those steps, especially as regards fingering, counting, tone, pedaling, efficiency, and memorizing.

Fingering Can Make or Break a Piece

There are three rudiments of piano playing that brook *absolutely no compromise of exactness* in practice. These are NOTES, FINGERING, and COUNTING. The student must be expected to take full responsibility for these rudiments once they have been explained, without the necessity for having them constantly policed at his lessons. Carelessness in their regard makes the conscientious teacher writhe, for he knows that any performance built on such a foundation has no more security than a house built with rotten lumber. The necessity for playing the correct notes is usually self-evident and rarely gives lasting trouble. The importance of precise, careful fingering and accurate counting, however, is not so clear to the student, who may continue to neglect either or both with nearly fatal consequences to the music and his control of it, until stringent remedial measures are taken. Unfortunately, the student who stems from inferior teaching almost invariably reveals carelessness and indifference in fingering and counting.

Perhaps the importance of fingering can be stressed further by quoting Emanuel Bach (see Source References) to the effect that it "is inseparably related to the whole art of performance." Not only did he cite the similar concern of his great father, but he gave extended space to the subject in his celebrated keyboard treatise, as Couperin had done before him and Türk was to do after him.

Our fingers are the means of contact between ourselves and the piano. All that we study and practice so hard is finally put into effect by these fingers. Which ones to use in what situations is the problem. As with the four main touch mechanisms in Chapter 2, the choice is like finding the right tool for a particular job. A disadvantageous choice of fingers means inefficiency if not actual failure in speed, power, and control. The best leverage applied by any of the four mechanisms can be undone in this way. Thus, the choice of and adherence to a fingering on a keyboard instrument can make or break a piece. It can profoundly affect memorizing, stage poise, technical mastery, speed of learning, and general security at the piano. Only among stringed instruments does the matter of fingering assume equivalent proportions. In wind instruments, it reduces itself to a relatively small number of clearly defined alternatives.

Why, then, is fingering so commonly neglected? The best answer is probably that the student is not compelled to use any one fingering in order to play the right notes, at least to play them after a fashion. He soon discovers that he can get by without reading the editor's fingering—if, indeed, he even notices that it is there. To be sure, by dint of repeated playings he does quickly fall into some sort of fingering that becomes habitual with him. But there lies the rub. The fingering he falls into is almost certain not to be the best fingering. Experimentation is required to discover the technical superiority of one fingering over another, and over-all planning is required to make the fingering consistent.

The ideal solution to careless fingering and the most constructive approach, in any case, is to have the student work out his own fingering, starting almost from the first piece he plays. He should get going on this task just as soon as he has given his new piece enough readings to get the general idea but not enough readings to establish bad habits. (And a word of caution is needed here, because bad habits of fingering have a way of establishing themselves with remarkably few playings, only to reappear in a most agonizing manner and on the most unexpected occasions.) I should like to urge that as much as the first quarter of the time spent on learning a new piece be devoted to a full consideration and final selection of the best possible fingering. The close study that will be entailed, with the hands considered separately and the music examined by sections, is, in fact, the best possible insurance that the new piece will have a rock-bottom foundation. Furthermore, it is my belief that the fingering brought in by the student should be a primary concern in the first lessons on each new piece, at which time it may be possible to show him still further and more practical solutions.

As to how the student goes about his fingering, some remarks may be offered that should prove useful. (Detailed illustrations are provided on pages 182–187, and principles for fingering scales, arpeggios, double-notes, and other drills were given in Chapter 3.) First of all, it would be best if he could play from editions that have not already been fingered by the editor. Then he could reach his own decisions without prejudice. However, the majority of editions do have fingering, the notable exceptions being most *Urtext* editions and some recent publications, especially those from France. The student's attitude when he encounters editorial fingerings should be one of interest and hard skepticism. The editor's fingering may represent enormous valuable experience, as it does, for example, in Joseffy's edition of Chopin. But more often than not it represents the hasty work of a dollar-a-page man—the kind who edits repeated passages differently and omits the fingerings that are the most problematic; or it represents the fingerings of a man with a hand of a different size and with different notions as to how such fundamentals as the trill, the chromatic scale, and repeated notes are to be played.

In any case, the student should try out systematically every possible fingering that he can find, including whatever the editor has to offer as but one possibility. Often he can discover the best solutions by working back from the end of a passage, just as a writer of mystery stories may work back from the end of a plot. If, after considering the various determining factors, he finds no one best fingering, then an arbitrary decision must be made. The problem is not so much to find one particular, "best" fingering as to find a good, usable fingering to which he can adhere faithfully.

When the student has decided upon a fingering, he should, without fail, *write it in,* with each number, small but clear, placed unambiguously near the note it concerns. A sharp pencil with a good eraser is recommended, but not a pen, which discourages erasures and later improvements. The fingering does need to be written in, both for the obvious reason that it would otherwise be forgotten in practice and for the less obvious one that written fingering is a great expediter when the piece is relearned at a later time. Fingering is more than an advantage for relearning; it is a virtual necessity. The habit of a particular fingering sticks much better than the recollection of it. When a pianist tries to relearn a piece that he failed to finger in writing on the first learning, he usually finds himself struggling to master different fingering that fights against the old habits he cannot recall.

Just how much fingering to put in requires good judgment, too. If every note is figured, the fingering becomes a major obstacle in reading. The rule should be to put in fingering wherever and only wherever there can be any chance of ambiguity, then or later. The student tends to put too much fingering in passagework and too little in chords and chordal accompaniments. If the right-hand thumb lights on c' and the passage progresses diatonically up to g', there is normally no need to put in anything but 1 for the thumb. He may assume, that is, that the fingers will succeed each other in their natural order and a note at a time unless fingering is put in to the contrary. Thus, if the same c' were fingered with the second finger, at least one other figure would be needed to show the way up to g'. Chords give the impression that no choice of fingering is possible. Actually, there is very often an alternative between 3 and 4 or 4 and 5 that directly concerns the ease of playing. A common instance is the waltz (*um-pah-pah*) accompaniment, in which the fifth finger of the left hand is often best saved for the bass while the other fingers play the afterbeats with the fingering that comes nearest to enabling both bass and afterbeats to be stretched as one chord. This fifth-finger bass, incidentally, can be aimed more accurately by approaching it as though the thumb were to play the octave above, too, and eying not the fifth finger but the thumb.

From what has been said, the importance of sticking to a fingering after it has been worked out must be apparent. Occasionally, more familiarity with the fingering will bring out unanticipated difficulties, necessitating changes that are hard to get used to. However, the student may prepare somewhat for such contingencies by testing his fingering both for more strength and more speed than he is likely to need in performance. In planning his fingering, he must realize that the ultimate speed may mean not only a greater but also a different technical problem. For instance, in Example 38 (from Ravel's "Scarbo"), the lower, standard fingering for a diminished-seventh arpeggio works well enough up to fast speeds. But for the almost instantaneous flash that Ravel expects, the upper fingering becomes well-nigh indispensable, the break between fifth finger and thumb being inaudible at that speed.

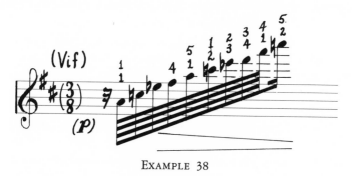

EXAMPLE 38

A major factor in the practicability of a fingering is its simplicity. Over and over again, a complex fingering that plays neatly and cleanly when the section is isolated becomes a mental hazard to concentration and memorizing when the piece is played through.

An example is the clever fingering of turns and other ornaments that is often recommended, apparently on the theory that the more different fingers that participate, the more articulate the results (as in 1–4–3–2–1 for a five-note right-hand turn starting on the main note). However, the simpler fingerings usually prove to be safer and surer (as in 2–3–2–1–2 for the same turn, even when the thumb is on a black key, or 3–2 or 3–1 for a trill, not 1–3–2–3 or other busy alternatives).

Another example is the exchange of two fingers on a single note, often on each of several single notes, in order to achieve a legato that might come more easily by sliding, adroit pedaling, or some other means. Another is the habit of changing fingers on repeated notes in slow to moderate tempos, when one finger propelled by a locked arm or even the trunk would prove to be much simpler to control. Still another example occurs in the sequential repetition of a short melodic pattern. The fingering that works well at one point in the sequence does not work so well at another. Nevertheless, the mental security gained by not having to watch for the finger change usually outweighs the slight advantage of the better fingering. Scale and arpeggio passages should ordinarily follow the standard scale and arpeggio fingerings to avoid confusion. One is inviting trouble, for example, by playing a right-hand scale in A major with 1–2–3–4 1–2–3 rather than the usual 1–2–3 1–2–3–4 unless something else about the passage makes this change necessary.

> For an interesting demonstration of how helpful a clear and simple mental concept can be, try two different fingerings for the four-note figure that keeps repeating in the cadenza at the end of Chopin's familiar Nocturne in E-flat (Example 39). The lower fingering looks right but becomes a tongue-twister as the cadenza speeds up. The upper fingering looks preposterous but becomes ideal once the shape of the cluster is realized and once the fingers are discovered simply to be succeeding each other *in their natural order,* 2–3–4–1–2–3–4–1–, and so on.

EXAMPLE 39

A second factor in practical fingering is the use of the strongest fingers for the strongest accents in the meter or other groupings. Thus, among numerous fingerings illustrated in Chapter 6 are uses of both the thumb and fifth finger on black keys at either end of an arpeggio figure. However such fingering may look or feel, it provides excellent strength and security on the extreme notes and few or none of the humps that might be expected with so brazen a defiance of the old rule about avoiding the thumb on a black key. That rule, by the way, still casts its shadow on pianists' fingering, wrongly discouraging them from many very sensible uses of the thumb for strength and accuracy. Thus, the thumb can save the day by rapid slides from black to white keys (as in the chromatic scales in double-notes illustrated in Chapter 3) or by covering adjacent keys in wide chords (as in Example 8, page 59). And, pointed down with fingers clenched, it can transmit arm attacks to a single bass tone that are too much for the fifth finger (if not the string!). Both the choice and the strength of fingering are also affected by decisions as to which hand should be marked "over" or "under" when one of them crosses the other or straddles it (as happens often in Debussy and Ravel).

A third factor in good fingering is consistency. Similar passages ought normally to be fingered similarly if the performer does not want to do twice as much work. Besides, if he does finger them differently he will find that the similar passages confuse each other in performance, meaning that the performer must be constantly on guard to remember which time he intended which fingering. Naturally, some latitude must be allowed, because the similar passages are often not so similar that identical fingering can be used. But then the very difference in the passage helps the pianist to remember the difference in the fingering, and conversely. In fact, there is even an occasion when he might deliberately use an altogether different fingering. That happens when one passage leads back to the beginning again and the same or a similar passage leads on to a new section, as often happens in a rondo. Then the alertness required to change the fingering is a wise precaution. (I recall how the excellent Viennese pianist Severin Eisenberger, while playing one of several recitals that covered the thirty-two Beethoven sonatas, started to go round and round at just such a passage in the "Rondo" of the *Sonate facile*, Op. 49, No. 1, finally giving up and walking off in exasperation!)

One other factor in practical fingering is the number of successive notes that can be covered ahead of time. Other things being equal, it is wise to have the fingering cover as many of the coming notes as possible in one grasp of the hand. As many as seven different *pitches,* which may recur to make many more *notes,* can be "covered" if two fingers do double duty, as illustrated on pages 184–185. The main point is always to have at least one finger that stays in place as a pivot or point of reference. This covering of more notes reduces the number of thumb shifts and promotes that streamlined, well-planted, solid style of playing sometimes known as position technique (related to the practice of clusters, previously discussed under Technique). Such fingering will often contradict the interruptions that editors deliberately make in fingering (for

example, ascending on the white keys by 3–4–5 2–3–4) so as to compel the separation of slurs and phrases.

Counting and Rhythm as Clues to Authoritative Playing

Others have said it, and here it is again: "In the beginning there was rhythm." One might add, "Everybody complains, but nobody does anything about it." One of the most important musical subjects is also one of the most elusive; hence the dearth of careful studies on rhythm, the frequent glossing over when it must be mentioned in other studies. (Here I hasten to interject: Neither is this the much-needed new study.) Rhythm, the coequal of pitch as one of the two essentials of music, seems to underlie all musical problems. Somewhat the way many apparent physical ailments prove to stem from psychosomatic problems, many apparent faults in technique, interpretation, and memory prove to stem from rhythmic problems.

It is surprising, for example, to discover how much the metronome alone will cure when used not for Maelzel's or Beethoven's original purpose, to set the tempo more precisely, but rather to regulate the counting. The teacher wears himself out trying to correct this quirk and that hesitation in his student, yet the minute one fault rights itself another appears, as if the problem were to

repair the oft-cited leaky bag. At last he thinks of the metronome, the student works with it, begins to get the swing of the music, and everything clears up like magic. I have known it even to help violinists with their intonation, since by clarifying the rhythmic direction it also clarifies the harmonic direction.

The metronome is often condemned, incidentally, by those who fear the mechanical results it will produce. There is a danger of mechanization, without a doubt. But let this much be said: The student who cannot and does not practice with the metronome up to the point where he can stay with it—and that is usually all he needs to do—faces the far greater danger of not understanding what he plays at all. As a sort of robot teacher during parts of the practice session, the metronome is a must for every serious student in spite of its relatively high purchase price. (Handy students can have fun and save money by making a simple electronic battery type, as explained in *Popular Electronics* for January 1969.)

The single most important thing the student can do about his rhythm, from the practical standpoint of this book, is to count. He should count the meter aloud in clear, crisp tones—not chant in weird, sustained tones, because then he is not defining the beats. He should not subdivide the beat with "ands" unless the tempo is actually so slow as to need subdivision—that is, where the use of "ands" is essential to the flow of the protracted beats. Otherwise, "ands" break up the beat, lose the sense of flow, and so defeat one important purpose of counting. Only when there is an irregular subdivision of the beat, as with dotted rhythms or the long and short notes of a triplet, may it be necessary to fill in the subdivisions temporarily. Thus, the student might count *one-de-de-de* to locate ♩♪ or ♫♪ correctly, but only on the beats where these occur. Such subdivisions often suffer distressing neglect. How ruinous to the heart of the rhythmic structure is the conversion of triplets into ♫♪ or dotted patterns into ♪♪ !

Quite apart from the noise and visual distraction, tapping the foot does not answer as a substitute for counting aloud both because the foot must be free to pedal, and to pedal independently of the rhythm, and because the voice can keep track of the position in the measure by numbering the beats. The student objects to counting aloud because "it mixes me up." But, of course, that exactly is the problem! The one rule governing the question when to count is simply this: The student must count everything he plays until he can say every count without confusion; then the counting has done its work. But he must be on the watch for absentminded mumbling in the place of counting or for the occasional omission of a count, for these are not accidents but positive symptoms of rhythmic confusion and lack of control.

The reason for counting must be understood. The student must realize that effective rhythm depends on the opposition of two factors, (1) the underlying pulse or beat and (2) the pattern of notes that is superimposed on that pulse. If he taps his foot while he whistles "Stars and Stripes Forever," for instance, he will note how the foot gives the pulse while the whistling sounds the pattern. To turn this fact into practice—that is, to play with *rhythmic authority*—he must be able to feel both pulse and pattern simultaneously. This is what is accomplished by counting (the pulse) aloud while playing (the pattern).

The student understands why he must get the pattern right (although he often has to be shown what "feeling it" means). So much he sees on the printed page and plays with his fingers. But he is likely to fall down on the counting unless this is supervised. The counting represents a pulse of definitely physical origin—a steady throb that takes place in the involuntary visceral muscles, so we are told. The act of counting aloud must be regarded as an exaggeration of what the student will later say to himself and of the pulse that he will come to feel inside. Mr. Loesser, who never failed to infuse his playing with rhythmic vitality, adds here:

> I have found it useful to tell students to think of music not as a bunch of notes arranged into a rhythmic pattern but rather as a skeleton of beats on which the notes are set, like the jewels on

a sunburst. A note may be defined as something that fits on a beat, a sound that must be placed on its own exclusive *time-spot*. First come beats, then notes.

Another useful suggestion is that instrumental music is, basically, dance music. For the most part it must sound "dancy," slow movements as well as fast; if it doesn't, it will sound unhappy. Playing in time is not a penance or even a discipline; it is just fun, just dancing.

Setting the pulse properly means getting into the *swing* of the music. We see this swing in the extreme when the jazz band leader sets the beat, before his men start in, by jogging at the shoulders and knees. A sense of swing can usually be trained—or rather, brought out—though students differ extraordinarily in their sense of pulse. (A student weak in rhythm often shows this weakness on the dance floor or in the marching band.) The overly shy, inhibited student is at a disadvantage because he is often reluctant to express himself in the energetic, muscular manner that the swing of the music requires. He must be helped to understand that whatever may be the merits of shyness in other living, piano playing is one activity where that shyness must be circumvented.

Undoubtedly, the physical interpretation of rhythmic patterns and pulses through Dalcroze Eurhythmics or similar dance movements helps to alleviate rhythmic apathy. Just how much it actually carries over to the problems of piano playing is hard to say. In any case, the student who succeeds in feeling and controlling the pulse in conjunction with the rhythmic pattern, who succeeds in bringing his rhythms to life, may congratulate himself on graduating from the large mass of pianists who play dully and indifferently because they play without this rhythmic authority.

Although many teachers will agree that a fair share of their energies goes into getting across the pattern ♩ ♪ and similar basic patterns, the fact remains that most children of five and six can learn to count the principal note values. A simple method of accustoming the student to the interrelation of the metric pulses and the note values in a new piece is to have him count the pulse aloud and clap the notes wherever they occur. This is fun for him and comes close enough to the actual experience of playing the piece to apply directly. If he continues to distort the values, a further help is to have him memorize the pattern of a specific passage, then both walk and count the pulse as he claps that pattern. Any tendency to totter in the walking is a sure sign that the problem of pulse-versus-pattern is not yet worked out. The metronome may accomplish the same purpose, of course, though the physical nature of the pulse will not then be so apparent to the student.

The most complex patterns to figure out mathematically—and figured out they must be, without fail—are those with many black notes, flags, beams, double-dots, and ties, such as are found in slow rather than fast movements. Familiar examples are the introductions to Beethoven's *Grande Sonate pathétique* and Liszt's Hungarian Rhapsody No. 12. Students also have difficulty in distinguishing the two or more sets of rhythms that belong to up- and down-stem melodies written on the same staff. They must figure these out, of course, in order to know how long each finger holds its note. The most complex patterns to do in performance are those with constant metric changes and energetic syncopations, as in the faster, dancelike movements of Aaron Copland.

Time signatures are like fractions, best translated into "this many (numerator) of these (denominator) in a measure," the numerator telling the number of pulses and the denominator the value of each. Thus, to translate $\frac{3}{4}$ the student only needs to say, "There are *three quarters* (fourths) in a measure." This method suffices for *simple* meters but must be amplified for *compound* meters, in which the denominator is compounded by threes in all but the slower tempos. The distinction between simple meter, with its pulse that subdivides by twos, and compound meter, with its pulse that is always dotted and subdivides by threes, is something all too many musicians fail to get clear. A small problem is created because the denominator of the simple time signature indicates the pulse whereas that of the compound time signature, except at the slowest tempos, indicates the (triple) subdivisions of the pulse, which, of course, would be too fast to feel as pulses, in any case. (Try walking each 8th-note in "Sailing, sailing, over the bounding main," which is in $\frac{6}{8}$ meter!)

To recognize compound time signatures, merely look for the numerators that are exactly divisible by three more than once. To translate such signatures all the way, merely divide the numerator by three and multiply the denominator by three, remembering that the denominator is a fourth or an eighth, and so on, not four or eight. Thus, $\frac{9}{8}$ or $\frac{6}{4}$ at moderate to fast tempos really means ♪· or ♩· . (Beethoven himself had trouble with this problem. Can you translate the $\frac{36}{64}$ that he seems to have meant when he put $\frac{12}{32}$ in the course of the finale of his Sonata in C minor, Op. 111?) Our present system of metric notation has no other means, aside from triplet signs, of indicating regular pulses with triple subdivisions. But think what delightful rhythmic types compound meter has produced, whether we single out the gigue at a fast tempo (as in the last dance of Bach's *French Suite* IV in E-flat), or the tarantella at a very fast tempo (as in Liszt's colorful *Venezia e Napoli III*), or the siciliana at a leisurely tempo (as in the poignant "Andante" from Mozart's Piano Concerto in A, K. 488). "Cut time," or *alla breve*, is unusual in being a compound meter, indicated by the signature ¢ or $\frac{2}{2}$, in which the pulse has a duple subdivision. Irregular meters imply irregular pulses with different subdivisions, as the signature $\frac{4+2+3}{8}$ implies in Bartók's first "Dance in Bulgarian Rhythm" (*Mikrokosmos* No. 148).

The physical nature of rhythmic feeling is important in another respect besides pulse, or rather in another aspect of pulse, which is tempo. Tempo means rate of speed. It is one more of those very elusive elements in rhythm—so elusive, in fact, that many have despaired of writing about it. In our fifth chapter some clues are offered for finding the most appropriate tempo in any one piece.

The problem is to determine just how fast Mozart intended a certain andante movement to be, or Scarlatti a certain presto movement, or at least approximately how fast Bach wanted his many compositions to be that contain no tempo designations at all. So it is that the one thing for which a pianist, conductor, or other performer may often be criticized with impunity is his tempo in this or that composition.

Of course, much of the music written later, in the nineteenth and twentieth centuries, is supplied with metronome speeds by the composer, and most earlier music is so marked by modern editors. These indications are indeed specific, but they present three main hazards or shortcomings. First, they are often open to question both because composers (Beethoven among them) are notoriously bad guessers as to exactly what tempos best suit their music and because the editor represents, after all, just another man's judgment. Second, they give a mechanical idea of speed but fail entirely to impart the physical feeling for the particular tempo. And third, they are too specific, because the tempo must depend somewhat on the prevailing mood, the occasion, the place, the instrument, the audience, and even the temperature. (For instance, the time required for sound to travel through the air may necessitate a slower tempo in a very large room than in a small room.)

To a seasoned orchestral conductor I am indebted for a very musical way to arrive at the five basic tempos of music, which may be designated as adagio, largo, andante, allegro, and presto. These five terms originated in Italian, among many others of similar intent, as designations for styles of physical movement from very slow to very fast. They may be translated as very slow, slow, moderate, fast, and very fast, though without giving any hint of their psychological character. As used by the great composers, they are ordinarily more meaningful than metronome markings. Each tempo may be *felt* by associating it with a familiar walking step, as is indicated in the following table. (Unfortunately, the meanings of adagio and largo are sometimes interchanged, and the other terms have often been used with varying intentions, but the sense of this discussion still applies.)

TABLE OF TEMPOS

Adagio. The delayed step done in a funeral march, down the aisle at a wedding, or at a graduation procession. So slow that it must be divided, in order to avoid faltering, by holding each foot back until it rises to its ball-of-the-foot at the middle of the count. Count with "ands" in order to subdivide the beat. Example: the "Funeral March" (marked "Lento," which is often equivalent to adagio) from Chopin's Sonata in B-flat minor.

Largo. The regal, sedate step used at a stately ceremonial or in the walk of a condemned man. As slow as can be taken without faltering or subdividing. Count one for each beat, without subdivision. Example: Dvořák's "Largo" from the *New World* Symphony.

Andante. The relaxed step used in a leisurely Sunday afternoon stroll or a Fifth Avenue window-shopping tour. Moderate and flowing, done without lifting the heel. Count one to each beat. Example: the "Andante cantabile" from Tchaikovsky's Fifth Symphony.

Allegro. The brisk step of a businessman walking to work on time but not late; in between the marching cadence of army troops and of most football bands. It is characterized by its spring and energy, sometimes including a takeoff from the ball of the foot. Count one to each beat (or each metric unit in cut time). Example: Brahms's Rhapsody in G minor.

Presto. When counted one to a beat, a short, mincing step taken almost at a run, as by a puppet or mechanical doll. So fast that it can be done only on the toes

> and with straight legs. Count one to an entire measure in simple time, one to a dotted unit or entire measure in compound time, up to the number of measures in a phrase or shorter grouping. Example: Mendelssohn's "Spinning Song."

These five tempos can be interrelated best by centering them around andante as the middle tempo. Andante should not be viewed on the slow side simply because it happens to be the designation for the slowest movement in many sonatas and other cycles. Returning to andante as a reference mean, compare the next slower tempo and the next faster tempo. Then approach adagio as being so slow that the beat has to be subdivided and presto as so fast that the beat has to be compounded.

An interesting and revealing sign of rhythmic insecurity is the bobbing of the head that many students will do when they are hard pressed to stay with the metronome or preoccupied with some difficulty in the notes. This is a bad habit that must be eliminated both by direct criticism and by tracing the rhythmic deficiency. It usually indicates that the player is trying to make up for a hitch that is upsetting the regularity of the pulse. In what was at the time a most humiliating experience, the wrongness of this habit was firmly impressed on me. I was still in my teens when I was invited to play a Handel harpsichord concerto with the Cleveland Symphony Orchestra (the "harpsichord" provided at that time being no more than a "prepared" Steinway with metal-tipped hammers). At the first rehearsal, I showed up with all the cockiness of inexperience. As soon as the first downbeat landed, I commenced all manner of energetic bobbings so as to keep pace with the conductor and the orchestra. It was only a matter of minutes before Nikolai Sokoloff, then the conductor, tapped his desk, stopped the orchestra, and slowly turned around to bellow, "What are you trying to do? Lead the orchestra?" Thoroughly chagrined, I telephoned the assistant conductor that night to learn what I had done wrong. The reply was simple. Orchestra players quickly learn

that head and body movements *on the beat* usually betray something unmusical going on *off the beat;* furthermore, those movements tend to throw other players off the beat and produce a muddy
ensemble.

Generally speaking, such movements in excess of technical requirements are like all mannerisms in performance, including
facial grimaces, breathy grunts, and flopping arms. They attempt to
make up for something not quite achieved in the music itself.
Furthermore, they are distracting to the audience, which usually
admires the quiet, businesslike performer who lets the music speak
for itself. It is worth noting that at the most intense and dramatic
moments performers sit fairly still, anyway, because they are too
busy to move about and because they dare not shift the base for
their aim, so to speak.

There are, however, a few occasions when rhythmic movements
by the head or body seem more justified. An experienced player
may make a slight buoyant or lilting movement from within the
trunk as he figuratively dances along with the beat. Or he may
jerk his head on a missing beat, as in a syncopation, which tempts
even the listener to reach out empathically and supply that beat. If
a rhythmic player must beware an occasional audible grunt at such
places, an arrhythmic one must be urged to do his "loudest playing"
on tied notes, dots, and rests, always recalling that such rhythmic
life presupposes alert, not slumped, posture.

Furthermore, in very slow music, where there is a problem of
keeping the flow going throughout the phrase (especially during
rests), the player might try making just one steady clockwise circle
for each phrase to and fro from the hips. In part, this circle replaces
the curlicues and dips of the baton that a conductor makes at slow
tempos in order to keep the beat flowing and to avoid delayed,
abrupt strokes that would take his players by surprise. But more
important, it implements a broad sense of direction that transcends
the beats and even the barlines at a tempo that could easily obscure
the directions otherwise. Students should be encouraged to make

such circular rotary movements when they show an inclination to fidget or to be bored with their own playing. Too often they tend to speed up and to miss the meaning of the long, even line of the phrase. Unfortunately, just as the art of writing noble, sustained slow music seems to be on the wane (though there are some heartening recent exceptions), so the art of playing it seems to be disappearing. No doubt the pace and intensity of our everyday living have something to do with this loss, for the audiences are similarly losing their patience with slow movements. If such should actually prove to be the trend, there could hardly be a worse loss to music!

Touch and Tone—Fact and Fancy

Touch, tone, and pedaling, which figure here as important concerns of Practice, might also have been included under Musicianship, for they are skills that rarely reach perfection among unmusical performers, or under Technique, because they depend so much on the control of the basic mechanisms. Here I insert a valued comment supplied by the eminent American composer and pianist Arthur Shepherd, who argues for an approach to these problems that is almost entirely by way of the musical senses:

> I have never been greatly interested in *theories* of piano technique. The *mechanics* of the thing I find rather boresome. To "lift or not to lift," to "rotate or not to rotate"—why labor such banal problems?
>
> This brings me to a note out of my own experience. I am a firm believer in the *empirical* approach. Piano playing, I believe, becomes a subtle, sensitive interplay of psycho-physical attributes. Touch, tone, tactility are all governed by a divining *ear*. Without the interplay of these factors or in the absence thereof, the piano is, I feel, the *worst* of all instruments.
>
> In my piano playing days I discovered over and over again that the way through a technical problem was by *ear!*

Oh, I don't mean to say that a conscious physical analysis is not incidentally to be reckoned with, but I do mean to say that the controlling and directing ear or aural faculty is too often forgotten, undeveloped, or left out of account.

How many pianists, do you suppose, have the well developed faculty of *hearing* sensitively and objectively what they are playing? With singers, the question is even more crucial.

Nowadays, in our mechanistic-ridden life we can and do fall back on disc and tape recordings to reveal the result of our doings. How much more important is the ability to coordinate our faculties on the basis of sound musicianship without exteriorizing the mechanics or spoiling the game by a priori theorizing?

A great deal has been written and said about touch, tone, and pedaling. Much less needs to be stated here, and much of that only to right certain misconceptions.

A starting point must be the instruments we play. Everything that was argued in the past two chapters about the control of the main touch mechanisms or levers and everything that needs to be added here about control will be meaningless if the piano to be used is itself beyond control. A piano will be beyond control if it is too inferior in construction to respond or if its action is decidedly out of regulation. Judging the quality of a piano is not only a matter of trying it to learn how it feels and sounds. It also calls for the opinion of an experienced piano technician, who can tell you about materials, repairs, and regulation. A proper regulation will need the services of that technician, too, because the skill required is quite the equal of that required to tune and regulate a modern auto properly. (Getting a member of the Piano Technicians Guild should give some assurance of expertise in a field that, alas, has its own share of charlatans.)

If the average pianist today has neither the training nor the equipment to do his own regulating (he is more likely to invest in something like a Strobotuner to do his own tuning), he does have a way to determine whether and when his instrument actually needs the regulating. There are three easy tests that he can make that will give at least a general indication. If the piano has been used extensively without a major action regulation in the last five years or so (costing from $100 to $125 in today's prices), it is all too likely to fail all three tests, I regret to say. As described here, the tests refer mainly to a grand piano and to the view one can get of its insides by removing the music rack. The first test is to observe the escapement, or "let-off point," in each hammer's travel up to the string as its key is pressed down very gently. That point should be about an eighth of an inch short of the string and about the same for each hammer. If it occurs too soon, the response becomes less predictable; if too late, it will tend to block the tone or even produce a most disconcerting double-strike.

The second test, using a ruler or similar aid, is to press and hold down about a dozen keys at once and at a moderate volume. This time observe whether the hammers are all caught (by the "back-checks") about halfway in their return fall from the strings to their rest points. If they fall to very different levels or simply rebound up again, it becomes impossible to do rapid repetition. And the third test is to strike each key in turn at a moderate volume and release it slowly while you observe whether its hammer rises from its halfway point as much as a quarter of an inch before completing the remainder of the fall to its rest point. If not, you have another indication (in the "repetition spring") that the all-important repetition action is failing. (In a contrary test of the same sort, one can release each key suddenly rather than slowly to see whether the hammer not only falls briskly but even bounces slightly off the rest point. If not, there is likely to be friction that should be eliminated in the hammer "flanges.")

As is generally known by now, the word *touch*, which is intimately bound up with the word *tone*, is something of a misnomer. The thesis has been established beyond reasonable challenge, a few diehards notwithstanding, that the style of striking the key cannot affect the timbre that results, whether the striking agent be a brick, a kitten's paw, or a human finger. (Mr. Loesser remarks, in this connection, that he likes to show how the right hand of Chopin's well-known Nocturne in E-flat major can be made to sound at least as well with a pencil, preferably one provided with a noiseless eraser, as with the naked finger.) Beyond the fraction of a second in which it strikes, the hammer simply has no further contact with the string. Consequently, one hardly need add that common statements like "she has a lovely touch" and impressive acts like the effort to produce a vibrato after the key is struck represent basic misconceptions.

What, then, produces the *illusion* of touch or the sense of tone production? Mostly one thing, and that is the relative volume or weight of the tone. By *relative* I mean the volume of one tone as compared with any other tones being sounded. For example, play the lyrical chord line that announces the main theme in the first movement of the Schumann Concerto, giving equal weight to all tones. The result will be dull and nondescript. Now play the same passage with each top chord tone appropriately emphasized and an illusion of "touch" results. I may seem to oversimpify, yet I might even add that to produce the renowned "singing tone" of Hofmann and others mainly means *hearing that each tone of a melodic line sounds over the accompaniment and right into the next tone*, especially each long-lasting tone.

The degree to which the melody tone should be brought out in chords naturally varies widely with the expressive intent of the music. However, inexperienced pianists commonly understate this tone by a considerable amount. They do not realize how clearly the tone can be projected before it sounds like forcing or even pounding. Remember that we are talking about relative, not absolute, weight of tone. Pounding rarely occurs when tones are played according to their relative importance, if the pedaling is clear and the capacity of the instrument itself is not exceeded.

To practice this tone production the student may distribute an eight-tone chord between his two hands and endeavor to bring out each tone in turn. His first step will be to extend the particular finger and play the desired tone slightly in advance of the others. When the teacher can detect which tone he means to bring out, the student is on the right track. Playing one hand louder than the other is ordinarily learned without difficulty. In strongly metrical music, however, the student may find that he is successful in subordinating the quieter hand only on the offbeats—that he is achieving no difference where the difference matters most, on the accented beats that the hands play together.

Five other factors also influence the illusion of touch or tone production and in some instances the actual quality of tone. One of these is certainly the degree of legato, discussed in Chapter 2. The more legato a melodic line is made, the longer each tone can be heard. (This slight extra length may even effect an enrichment of each tone if, as some argue, a tone's partials, or "overtones," require an appreciable moment of time to form.) Another factor is the use of the pedals, which not only may relate to the legato but in more than one way can affect the very structure of the tone, as will be discussed shortly. A third factor is the sense of direction imparted by intelligent phrasing, rhythmic grouping, and harmonic inflections. Although this sense of direction does not change the tone, it does have the psychological effect of calling more attention to it. A fourth factor is the negative one of any external noise that may be present. The noise can arise from squeaks in the action or sympathetic vibrations in the instrument or the room; or it can result from slapping on the key surfaces, thereby hinting at inefficient attacks that need to be remedied.

Finally, the primary factor that affects the actual quality of tone is its relative intensity, or volume. Although a pianist cannot affect the tone by his manner of striking the key, he does affect it when he changes its intensity. The quality of a piano tone changes from cloudy to bright as it grows louder, causing the high partials to figure more in the total sound. To be sure, this change is fixed at any one intensity by the quality and state of the instrument and is not alterable during performance. But a skillful pianist can exploit the change extensively through subtle nuance. He does this solely by controlling the speed of key descent. Full control of the key descent is possible only in music slow enough to allow time for that control. But, of course, it is in such music that tone production matters the most.

To control the key descent best, one must (1) employ only one touch at a time, avoiding any give at intervening joints and (2) start *from*, not above, the key surface in a prepared attack. Then he will be able to increase the speed of descent slightly but constantly as he sticks with the key right down to the bottom, or key bed. It is helpful to feel for the let-off point of the hammer just before the key bed is reached, the purpose being to maintain that continual contact with the key and hence the control over it. We encounter somewhat the same principle if we push a little boy in his coaster wagon. If we give just one abrupt shove, the wagon leaves us immediately and is out of our control. If, on the other hand, we begin in contact with it and gradually push faster, we continue to keep the wagon in control.

A useful exercise at this point is to play 20 eight-tone *tenuto* chords, gradually progressing from *pianissimo* to *fortissimo* on the eleventh chord and back to *pianissimo* (as in Example 40).

EXAMPLE 40

Try for one steady swell and diminish, not a zigzag pattern. The inexperienced pianist tends especially to diminish too rapidly after the eleventh chord, arriving at his *pianissimo* too soon, with no control left. The exercise quickly makes clear, if nothing else will, the advantages of using only one touch mechanism at a time and of the prepared attack. The mechanism in this instance might well be the trunk (locked in one piece right to the fingers) if the speed is not faster than about $\rfloor = $ M.M. 40. It is helpful to slide forward on the key slightly as it is "ridden" to the bottom of the key bed each time (perhaps helping to explain why some pianists actually prefer not to have their keys cleaned too close to performance time!).

To return to the key, the object of the controlled descent, as already indicated, is controlled intensity. However, once the tone is sounded, the pressure can and should relax. As Mr. Loesser effectively illustrates, any effort to maintain the contact after the tone is sounded merely taxes the student's "peace of mind and muscle":

> Students are constantly falling into the same illusion that afflicts telegraphers' apprentices: when the telegraph key makes its contact a buzz is heard; the young operator has the feeling that he is making the sound and presses hard. The "firmness of contact" that occurs is regarded as a very bad habit, leading to cramp and fatigue. The manuals on telegraphy warn against it very explicitly. Likewise, "firmness of contact" is to be avoided on the piano.

In spite of all the minute analysis that has gone into tone production in one publication after another, the mastery of key descent and release must become a matter of feel rather than intellect for the performer. In any case, as he gains increasing mastery of his skills, the matter of touch and tone becomes less and less a question of technique. The qualities of gentleness or stridence or thinness or fullness that we come to associate with particular artists of experience represent, primarily, differences of personality and temperament.

Do You Hear What You Pedal?

There is a reason why pedaling is a much neglected subject in piano study, a subject often only cursorily treated by the teacher and but little noticed by the student. Pedaling is a highly sensitive, almost nervous, art, dependent almost entirely on the ear of the performer. Students tend not to notice their pedaling because hearing, which should come first, all too often comes last among the many responsibilities that they must bear in mind. Sometimes they pedal merely to hide a multitude of sins, as the expression goes.

Unfortunately, the pedaling indications by past composers, especially from Haydn to Chopin, are likely to be controversial, partly because they seem to be so incomplete and partly because the instruments were so different. At best, editorial suggestions for pedaling are bound to be inadequate and misleading because good pedaling is a matter of the performance at any one moment—of the instrument, the location, and the mood of the player—and because good pedaling involves many more movements and half-movements and variations in timing than could possibly be indicated by an editor. In most instances, literal adherence to the editorial markings for the pedal will be practiced only by un-musical performers and can lead to many bad sounds.

Pedaling depends, of course, on style and color. The *damper pedal*, whose misuse is apparent in the popular designation "loud pedal," governs sonority. When it is pressed down, causing the dampers to rise off the strings, it makes for enriched tones through stronger partials—that is, by allowing the other strings in tune with its partials to vibrate sympathetically. The whole instrument seems to resonate. When the pedal is let up, the tone deadens correspondingly. The kinds of sonorities appropriate for Bach, Mozart, Liszt, and Debussy will differ widely (as illustrated more specifically on pages 191–192). In this matter of styles, the teacher can be of real help. Otherwise, beyond showing the how of a very few standard methods, like syncopated pedaling, his best help can be to remind and re-remind the student to hear what he plays.

Syncopated pedaling means the continuous, overlapping sort in which the foot lifts exactly as each new harmony is played, pressing down again to retain that harmony before the fingers release and while the next harmony is being approached. The procedure looks simple, but it is still largely a matter for the ear. As the tone gets lower in pitch, its vibrations last longer, meaning that it takes longer to clear in the pedaling. (Try connecting two successive loud octaves in the bass with syncopated pedaling. Then, while the pedal retains the second octave, press the first one down again *silently* and hold it, release the pedal, and you may be dismayed to discover the first octave still sounding.)

Low tones in broken chords are hard to catch in the pedal. Sometimes a low tone can be caught by the *sostenuto* (or middle) *pedal,* though the use of this pedal to retain only certain tones is seldom necessary or effective except in recent music where composers deliberately have allowed time for its operation. (Surprisingly, neither Debussy nor Ravel seems ever actually to have prescribed its use. And unfortunately, the sostenuto pedal can be counted on to function properly only in the best grand pianos.) Otherwise, the low tone must be held while the upper tones change harmonies. Then the ear must decide how much can be blurred, how much can be taken care of by "half pedals" (made possible by the fact that the higher vibrations die out more quickly), and how much must be lost. Blurring is an art, too.

> Indeed it is [Mr. Loesser adds]. For instance, a single unchanged harmony can endure a certain amount of impurity without unpleasantness, but any confusion of harmonies intended to be different is annoying. The amount of dissonance involved is not in itself the determining factor. Another thing: the psychological effect of the blur is determined by the amount of time it is given to sink into the mind. A blur rapidly obliterated is hardly interpreted as such, but rather as smoothness or legato. But relative loudness also affects the endurability of a blur. Play a few notes softly with the pedal down and let them die away to a *pianissimo*. There will be no harmonic impurity, merely a "color" effect. Now play some unrelated chords *forte* without changing the pedal. The criticism "too much pedal" must be carefully understood; usually it means "not enough pedals."

Blurring is out of place in Mozart but is often used with fine effect in Debussy and sometimes in Chopin. In chromatic, contrapuntal, or other music with kaleidoscopic, fluctuating harmonies, the pedal usually has to be applied in a tentative, flutter style. Contrary to frequent statements, so-called "half-" and "quarter-pedals" refer to partial releases, not partial applications (see the *Piano Quarterly* No. 29, p. 30). All too few pianists realize that inappropriate blurring will produce the illusion of a harsh touch quite, indeed, as will the opposite fault of inadequate finger legato.

With regard to the "soft" pedal, the problem is naturally somewhat less, since this pedal does not need to be changed as the harmony changes. Its first purpose is to provide an actual variation of timbre at a softer intensity. This purpose is achieved with better effect on a grand piano, where the slight lateral shifting of the keyboard and hammers eliminates one of the unison strings so as to leave but *due corde* or *una corda,* than on an upright, where the hammer stroke merely shortens. (On the modern grand piano, where three unison strings reduce only to *due corde,* it is not possible literally to follow Beethoven's request in the slow movement of his "Hammerklavier" Sonata, Op. 106, first for "una corda," then "poco a poco due ed allora tre corde.") The change of timbre results from string contact on a softer, ungrooved part of the felt hammer and from sympathetic vibrations by the eliminated unison string (which is now free to vibrate even where a "node" would be created otherwise by the hammer stroke). Sometimes this change is reserved only for Romantic and Impressionistic music, but it seems equally appropriate in Baroque or Classic music as the piano's modest counterpart to the shift from one register to another on the organ and harpsichord, or from *tutti* to *soli* in large instrumental ensembles. Pianists frequently resort to the soft pedal solely to produce softer playing than the technique of the pianist can otherwise produce. But purists may object to this use, saying that loud and soft playing, however delicate the latter, must always be under muscular control.

Practice Methods That Save Time and Effort

The quotation from Bacon at the beginning of this book is now commended to the reader who may weary of being told so often, in today's English, that we learn exactly what we practice. Three statements to this effect, thus far, are perhaps too many. Yet the principle, being a basic one, cannot help but reappear. It certainly should be ever welcome to the many would-be pianists who feel they are wasting time in practice. And that brings us to the text of the immediate discussion, which is efficiency in practice methods.

When Bacon wrote, ". . . if they be not well advised, [men] do exercise their faults and get ill habits as well as good," he could just as well have been referring to mistakes in piano practice. For, in brief, the pianist who makes mistakes in his practice learns them whether he means to or not. The viciousness of this fact may not be immediately apparent. To state it more fully, the pianist who makes a slip chalks it up to carelessness or to human error, or he merely calls it an accident. But the learning

process does not distinguish between accidents and conscious efforts. Whatever is done is learned and becomes a muscular coordination. Mistakes become learned and stick just as correct procedures do. In fact, old mistakes, even when they are corrected subsequently with great care, have a demonic way of turning up in public performance.

Every teacher knows the student who makes so many mistakes in his playing that he figuratively stutters at the piano, and he knows that the habit can be just about as hard to cure as stuttering. I remember a young lady in a conservatory who practiced doggedly, day in and day out, for several months, at Bach's Two-Part Invention in F minor. I began to listen to her when I noticed how every measure was peppered with trials and errors before the right notes appeared. Presently I realized that this was extremely successful practice, if not from the young lady's or Bach's standpoint, at least from the standpoint of muscular training; for every mistake that once had been an accident was now a thoroughly mastered, integral part of the piece, a part that could be counted on with certainty to appear each time the piece was repeated!

But, the student will argue, accidents are accidents, so what can I do? And the answer? You can do a great deal if you set your mind to it. Mainly you can catch yourself before you make the mistake, just as you would if you found yourself about to walk off a cliff or to run down a pedestrian. The fact must be granted, however, that catching oneself or anticipating the mistake in advance can be very difficult. The student who has fallen into the mistake habit is usually the type whom the momentum of the rhythm leads around by the nose. Once he is on the verge of a mistake, the rhythmic drive pushes him over, and he realizes his error too late. Too late, because even going back to correct the mistake does little toward counteracting the muscular coordination that has been practiced.

The cure for this habit often takes patience and time. First, the student must establish as his motto the words *Hesitate rather than err.* He should understand that mistakes stick, but hesitations of thought are easily bridged over in due time. They are, in fact, a normal characteristic in the early stages of any learning. Second, a corrective should be instituted, a corrective more painful to the student than the disturbance caused by his mistakes. One telling corrective, though certainly inefficient from other standpoints, is to begin a piece and start over every time the slightest slip of any sort occurs, even the kind that is truly a human error. After one gets almost to the end several times, and if the patience of student and teacher are not yet exhausted, the desire to get through the piece will usually overcome the momentum factor and bring home the value of hesitating rather than erring. The student will be helped, too, by actually hearing and seeing the teacher's demonstration of careful, cautious practice. (And he might look ahead at this point to the checklist of questions proposed on page 188.)

If the student *is* too late, and the mistake has already been learned, then he may try an interesting corrective recommended by psychologists and typists: Go back and make the mistake deliberately a time or two, the theory being that making an error consciously will rid it of its involuntary character by bringing it to the surface—that is, into the consciousness. Neither teacher nor student should encircle the mistake with a pencil. (One soon learns to recognize the age of such mistakes, like the age of trees, by the number of rings.) This method merely encourages the student *not* to be careful about what is *not* so marked! In summary, we can see the importance of intelligent concentration as against the brute force method of constant repetition, whose only advantage is that it does not tax the weary mind.

Learning is thought to represent the combining of a series of individual reflexes into one continuous or chain reflex, with each individual reflex setting off the next one. This concept leads to the question, often debated, as to whether it is better to practice from the whole to its parts or vice versa. Without getting into the more specific approach to be detailed in Chapter 6, I can report from my own experience that it is usually better to start with the over-all view so as to put the practicing into perspective— that is, it is better to go through the entire piece or movement and include everything at once, from fingering to dynamics, always remembering the value of hesitation as a means of ensuring accuracy. The hesitation makes it possible to think through one thing at a time before doing everything at once.

The student may still complain that there is too much to do at one time. But, again, if he does *not* do everything at once he is practicing incorrectly what he does practice. Then he will have the still greater problem of unlearning and relearning later on what he had only half practiced before. One cannot say, "Today I shall learn the notes, tomorrow the fingering, and the next day the dynamics," as though adding story upon story to the foundation of a new house. If the student needs an intermediate stage, the right answer is one-hand practice, which, in any case, should be a regular stage in his mastery of a new piece.

By going right through the piece from the start, the student will find that many easier problems take care of themselves in the course of several playings, leaving relatively few sections to be practiced separately as the piece nears completion. Small-section practice should serve largely as a means of final polishing. He who begins by trying to perfect the first line, then the next, and so on, usually ends up with the beginning sounding fine, the middle fair, and the ending weak, to say the least. If anything, the ending should sound best, since it leaves the last impression. By practicing the entire piece, beginning on page 3 on Tuesday if page 2 marked the end of Monday's practice, the effort will be evenly distributed.

After making some headway, the student is tempted to practice fast all the time. The danger here, however, is that the larger, chain reflex will begin to disintegrate if the individual reflexes are not continually renewed by slow practice. That is, after practicing only fast for a while, the student is surprised to find his piece falling apart instead of improving. Too much emphasis can hardly be placed on the need for slow practice as a means of concentrating *consciously* on the notes. It is by getting time to think them through that one both makes and restores the individual reflexes. Slow practice also permits free, exaggerated muscular action by whichever mechanisms are doing the playing, this action being another means of restoring the individual reflexes, although a means that must not be allowed to induce tightness. After the piece is securely learned, an average need is likely to be one time of slow to every two times of fast playing. Sometimes the habit of playing fast becomes so strong that the metronome must be used to hold down the tempo.

Of course, fast practice must not be ruled out. It is not only the way that the pianist will have to play his piece, but it is also a main way to eliminate waste motion (see pages 80–81). Such motion is the bane of high speed, as I can well remember in my prancing struggles to attain speeds that my teacher seemed to play effortlessly, as though he were just coasting. Some difficulties show up only at full speed. For example, only when Chopin's Prelude No. 16 in B-flat minor is played up to its whirlwind tempo, "presto con fuoco," does the pianist discover one of its prime difficulties. I am not referring to the obvious difficulty of the right hand's 16th-notes but to the follow-through motion required to play the three-note left-hand groups all in one sweep. Often it is not the student's technique so much as his imagination that limits his speed. He cannot conceive the larger swing of the more rapid tempo. Then something must be done to raise his sights. He may try letting the metronome pull him up to the fast tempo, or he may listen to a performance of the piece at that tempo.

Again, practice *what* and *only what* is needed. As the piece progresses, certain parts will prove to be much easier than others. In spite of the student's temptation to play most the parts he knows best, there is no point in practicing these every time the piece is played. Note how efficiently a successful conductor rehearses his orchestra. Since the professional rehearsal time is always expensive and brief, the conductor comes to the stand at the starting minute, taps for attention, and calls, "Gentlemen, start at letter *O* in the overture." He knows the men have played the music, that they will remember most of it readily, and that the chief trouble may occur at letter *O*.

If the pianist is maintaining a program of scales and other drills, he does best to distribute these throughout his practicing, where they will apply to specific pieces, rather than to exhaust himself by doing them all at once. The pianist will also do well to budget not only his daily time but the weeks and months that lie ahead. Experience will show him what he can expect of himself. By making a long-range schedule, he will have continual goals by which he can keep tab on his progress. Some pieces take much longer to mature than others, but this fact does not impose a moral obligation on the learner to live with every piece for months or even years before he plays it. Ravel's difficult *Tzigane* was reportedly played with splendid effect for the first time by a violinist who had mastered it in exactly three days! Too often, protracted study means inefficient study.

Sometimes the procrastinative student can help himself by submitting to his teacher a weekly written report of his practice and accomplishments. The teacher can also help by writing the student's assignment each week, along with specific criticisms, in a lesson notebook. In this way, the student finds himself "legally responsible" for the suggestions he has received. Even so, he had better review his lesson soon after he leaves the teacher in order to fix the many detailed suggestions that cannot be written down. Whatever his method, the student should realize that he is engaged in a kind of tortoise-versus-hare race with himself. His chances of winning out are far greater if he runs the careful, cautious course. If he is too tired or preoccupied to practice accurately when practice time comes around, then— even though it is a risky prerogative to offer the irresponsible student—he had better wait until he is thoroughly awake and able to concentrate. It is much harder to unlearn and relearn a piece that has been practiced carelessly than to begin it for the first time.

Is Memory Your Undoing?

Memorizing might properly have been included among the practice methods just discussed. It earns this niche all by itself, however, because it ranks among the pianist's chief concerns. About a fourth of those who get ahead in piano playing have very little trouble with memorizing. For the others, this skill— and it is indeed a skill—looms as one of the biggest obstacles to their prospects of being a "compleat" pianist. "If only I didn't have to play by heart!" or "I can manage the other things but I simply can't memorize my music!" These phrases must have a familiar ring to every teacher. Why, then, do we bother to memorize? Is memorizing just an affectation made mandatory by tradition? Affectation was the word used by some of Liszt's critics when he started to give public recitals from memory; it also has been used in reference to an increasing tendency among present-day orchestra leaders to conduct from memory. No, an element of affectation may sometimes be present, as is also the factor of tradition, but there are much better reasons for memorizing.

From the student's standpoint, memorizing is the best means

of ensuring that the notes get from the printed page into himself. It is second only to the fingering he works out as a way of compelling careful attention to detail. While perfect memorizing is no proof positive of complete understanding, it is at least evidence that all the minutiae have been perceived and recorded. From the performer's standpoint, memorizing is often a technical necessity. The success of certain blind pianists notwithstanding, most of us still need to eye the keyboard in the livelier passages, leaving little time to read a score. Liszt was hardly the first performer to play from memory, but one can understand from the wide leaps and extended range of his music why he found this manner of playing necessary.

Finally, memorizing is an undeniable advantage as well as a convenience to artistic playing. The elimination of note reading and page turning allows the performer to devote just that much more attention to his performance. It also permits the music to be called forth from inside oneself, as it were, so that the notes are assimilated before rather than while they are performed. One may argue that the fear of forgetting is at least as much of a distraction as page turning and note reading. The only answer is that if the piece is memorized thoroughly enough there will not be such a fear. One may also argue that most chamber music players still perform in public with their "notes." So they do, but the string and wind players do not need to watch their fingerboards or keys, and the pianist then has other reasons for needing the music in front of him. He must keep the full chamber music score under his view. Besides, as it happens, experienced performers of chamber music often find themselves playing for stretches at a time without glancing at their music.

It is well known that several kinds of memory contribute to secure memorization—among them, auditory, visual, touch, and intellectual memory. In actual practice, what do these mean? Auditory memory is the kind that enables us to hear what comes next in the music. Most performers have no difficulty remembering the approaching sound as they play along. But many of them cannot translate this sound into fingers and keys when they hit a snag. In other words—and here we go back to the first topic in this book—these persons cannot play by ear. They are the ones who tend to stop cold when something throws them off ("I don't know what happened; everything just seemed to go blank!"). By contrast, the performer who plays by ear can usually get near enough to the actual notes he hears to improvise his way out of his troubles or at least to improvise to a respectable cadence from which he can either go on or go back.

Visual memory is the kind that leaves us a mental image of the way the notes look on the printed page or, more commonly, the way they look on the keyboard. This kind of memory undoubtedly helps, but there is not much the student can do to further it. Any time spent trying to recall the look of the staff or the keyboard is probably much better spent on other, more positive or dynamic approaches to memorizing.

Touch memory is the sort that allows us to play the piece by physical feel and momentum. In other words, it is habit. It plays an important part in the automatic quality of continuous playing from memory, as does hearing. The habit on which touch memory depends is muscular coordination. Muscular coordination will be very secure if the music has been practiced accurately, sufficiently, and with the same fingering. Otherwise it will be insecure, with the chances for successful memorizing affected accordingly. Yet, at best, touch memory alone does not suffice for secure memorizing. The moment a slip occurs to throw the performer off the automatic track, he is lost, much as is the novice salesman who is interrupted in his prepared talk. Then other types of memory must be called to assistance.

Intellectual memory is the kind that results from a conscious knowledge of the music. Total reliance on it would, unfortunately, yield only what the reviewers condemn as a "studied" performance. Yet it is the kind with which the performer can do most on short notice and without which he will never feel secure. Anything that brings the music to the performer's consciousness contributes to intellectual memory, whether it concerns form, tonality, counting, technique, melodic line, or programmatic association. If he is observant when he practices, he will mentally record much about the music that will stand him in good stead.

This much is relatively painless. But most players should face the fact with courage—for courage is what deliberate memorizing takes—that a certain amount of ornery, tedious work is required to assimilate this knowledge securely. Such memorizing of the music must make sense to the performer. He must see the details in intelligible groups and patterns. A succession of dominants, a chord built in fourths, a series of three-measure phrases, a bass line that descends by two, a rondo design, a canonic progression—all of these are dependable aids to the player who discovers them. Furthermore, he is more likely to retain such relationships if he does discover them for himself than if they are simply passed on to him by the teacher.

Memorizing is discussed last in this chapter on practice methods only because the other topics need to be considered first in learning a new piece. However, that order does not mean that memorizing should be delayed until late in the mastery of a piece. The teacher who waits until the student can play the piece nearly perfectly to say, "All right, now go memorize it," is asking the student almost to relearn the piece. Of course, many students, especially the younger ones, will have just about memorized the piece by this time anyway. But the others will find that playing from memory is a very different experience from playing with the score before them. Memorizing was cited as a skill in its own right. Therefore, it must be practiced just like any other skill if there is to be any hope of relying on it in performance. The student should begin to play from memory as soon as the habits of fingering, counting, and interpretation are correctly planted. Even before this time, many a player likes to memorize the passages that are technically most difficult as a means of getting on with their practice.

To go about memorizing, the student's first step must be to dispense with the music once and for all, at least on the piano rack. Curiously, the habits of looking at the score and playing from memory fight each other. Not only may memorizing seem difficult when one is used to looking at the score, but, conversely, reading from the score becomes difficult after one gets used to playing from memory! In fact, students often note that they undo their hard-earned memorizing by returning to the score for a time. In other words, going back to crutches is no way to get rid of crutches.

Many students leave the music on the rack and merely try to avert their eyes from it. But then there is too great a temptation or unconscious inclination to peek. When it becomes necessary to recheck the score (as should be done periodically anyway if the

memory is not to go astray), it is much better to put the music
on top of the upright piano or far back on the grand piano so
that the student at least has to stand to refer to it. Then he will
try harder first to recall the note. A note recalled with such effort is
a note won by the memory. (At least in that sense, my own
memorizing has made the best progress when I have found myself
practicing some place with no score on hand at all!)

The student should work on a page or more at a sitting, dividing the music into logical sections. Doing too little or too much
at a time is inefficient. The amount his mind can encompass will
depend on the nature of the music and will increase as his piano
playing advances. Homophonic music usually takes hold quicker
than contrapuntal or extremely dissonant music. When he first
tries to play from memory, he is likely to get stuck very soon. If
he cannot recall the note, he should stand to check the score, try
to see the note in some sort of intelligible pattern, then resume just
before that point, *not at the beginning.* In this way, he may have
to stand twenty-five times before he completes the section, but he
will be surprised the next time to find that he has to stand only,
say, fifteen times. Five of those times may be to check spots that
he missed formerly, and the others to check new ones. Eventually
it may be that he will have to check nearly every note. Yet, in
its plodding way, though it may tire the standing muscles, this
system works—and works in a way that is fundamentally right
and efficient learning.

When the student returns to his memorizing the next day, he
should make certain that he begins with a new section, thus doing
his hardest concentrating while he is freshest. Moreover, he will
be furthering that over-all perspective stressed earlier. It does not
do to perfect the first section—"The boy stood on the burning
deck, The boy stood on the burning deck, . . ."—before going on
to the next, with no sense of the over-all interrelationships. In
any case, the old material will seem easier when he gets back
to it later in the practice session.

Last, among major helps toward clinching the memory work is counting from memory. The counting keeps track of the barline and all that that implies, both rhythmically and harmonically. Uncertain counting, like uncertain fingering, is sure to mean uncertain memorizing. Also, the student should have landmarks every few measures at logical cadential points in the music, where he can begin anew if he does get stuck. To make certain that these landmarks can be recalled on split-second notice, at the first sign of memory failure, he should practice skipping about arbitrarily from any one to any other. And it is a good idea to try the skipping about in the mind alone, away from the piano. In fact, it is excellent preparation to go through the entire work in that way, although the feat is certainly one requiring unusual powers of concentration. At least, the landmarks will stave off disaster until one gets to that rare point where he literally knows every note of the piece. To play from the beginning to the end of a piece without any such landmarks is like walking a tightrope from rim to rim of the Grand Canyon.

5. Performance

HAVING FOUGHT his way thus far along the tortuous road that leads to accomplished pianism, the student, like Tamino in *The Magic Flute,* is ready for his final test—performance. Performance requires perfection of the music and poise on the

stage. Both the perfection and the poise make for special problems, some of them interdependent, that will be considered presently. But first, some students may want to know why they should perform at all. Comparatively few students perform because they hope to have concert careers. The others, if they ever do perform, perform because their teachers present recitals, or their parents and friends ask them to play, or they themselves welcome the chance to show what they can do.

Is the teacher justified in putting on the recitals? Yes, for three reasons: the recitals mark periodic goals toward which the student can work, they afford unusual opportunities to view the student's work in perspective, and they provide performance experience. The last reason is often given as the first, though it may well be the least important one. Too much emphasis is usually placed on the experience in public performance that the recitals will afford. Recitals, well coached, do train the student in poise before an audience, but they are no assurance that every performance will go without a hitch. Much depends mainly on how well the music has been learned on each occasion. Even the most experienced pianists face disaster if they dare to appear without proper preparation, while a totally inexperienced student may "knock the sparks off" a piece that has been well learned.

Interpretation: The Sum of Understanding, Experience, and Talent

Music is one of the time arts. This classification means that, unlike the space arts—painting, sculpture, and architecture—music can and must be brought back to life by a new projection in time on every occasion that it is to be appreciated. There must be a middleman between producer and consumer who returns to the mute notation on the printed page in order to recreate the creations of the composer. This recreating is what is meant by interpretation. Its purpose, in short, is to convey the meaning and intentions of the composer, both expressive and intellectual. (For more on music as a time art, see Chapter 8 of my *Understanding Music,* listed in the Source References.)

Effective, convincing interpretation presupposes three attributes on the part of the interpreter: experience, understanding, and musicality or native talent. It will be understood, then, why interpretation seems like such an indefinable subject, why the teacher tends to stop at that point, saying to the student, "From here on, either you can or you cannot." Interpretation is really the intangible sum of *every*thing that goes to make up piano playing, including everything that is discussed here, for that matter. And it includes other things, too. It includes all that goes to make up personality, quite apart from problems of piano practice and performance, for out of our personality we get the predispositions that determine our tastes. In spite of a well-known statement to the contrary, notation is still only implicit rather than explicit, and a great deal in the matter of taste is left to the performer, even in the music most scrupulously edited by the composer. It is no wonder, then, that interpretations can differ so widely without losing their validity at either extreme. This latitude, which makes possible the continual refreshment of music (or any time art), is, in fact, one main reason why art remains beautiful, mysterious, and unchained.

Of the three prerequisites to effective interpretation mentioned, only understanding can be considered here. Actual experience and innate musicality do not come from a book. Over and above the basic knowledge required to read, count, finger, and manage the notes, there are certain more advanced aspects of understanding that matter particularly in interpretation. One is the understanding of form. Form includes whatever binds the music into a unified structure, whether it be tonality, rhythm, melody, or, as is usually the case, a combination of all three. The student's problem is to determine which of these predominates and how; or, to put it colloquially, What makes the piece tick?

He will not need a course in form and analysis, desirable as that would be, to discover the reiterations of a fugue subject, the return of a rondo theme, the digression in an A-B-A design, or the simple variation of a melody. Nor will he have undue difficulties in detecting varieties of rhythmic treatment. He *will* need at least a rudimentary foundation in harmony, which he needs anyway for his daily playing, to recognize the tonal scheme of a Haydn sonata or the three or four cadences in nearly related keys that outline a Bach invention. A further knowledge of harmony should increase his sensitivity to the pushes and pulls, the tensions and relaxations, that operate continually throughout the musical discourse. With what background and ability he has to perceive form traits, the student will benefit himself by jotting down in the score whatever he can find on his own. This analysis he might submit to the teacher for discussion, along with the fingering that has been worked out, at one of the first lessons on a new piece. True, the gist of his findings might eventually impress itself on his senses without the conscious analysis. But, how much easier for him, as for the animal seeking food in the psychologist's maze, if the right doors are opened in advance.

An understanding of form is an important means of arriving at a *concept of the whole* in performance, which is, strangely, one of the most neglected and yet one of the most vital aspects of interpretation. Even established performers will play through extended compositions with remarkable attention to detail and little or no sense of the broad interrelation of large sections. They will fail, for example, to perceive the climaxes on a comparative basis, or will lose track of the prevailing tempo, or do each return to a theme in the same manner, or make a sudden dynamic thrust, such as an extra-loud final chord, that is wholly out of keeping with the general level of the piece.

Here, as in other piano problems, the metronome may be of some help, for its use can pull together the over-all form of a piece that has a single or prevailing tempo by integrating its diverse rhythms. But this step is only the beginning. In Baroque keyboard music, before Haydn and Mozart—that is, before the time when composers generally put interpretative markings in their music—the student has an exceptional opportunity to advance an independent concept of the whole piece. For this purpose, he should use an *Urtext* edition, which will have few if any markings, or at the very least some edition in which he can recognize and, if need be, disregard the editor's additions. His problem will be to work out and enter intelligent, judicious decisions of his own on those interpretative factors that most help to illuminate the form, including dynamics, phrasing, and articulation. (Specific applications are illustrated and discussed on pages 176–181.)

With regard to dynamics, the student should realize that a continual series of short crescendos and diminuendos is by no means a guarantee of intelligent, musical interpretation. Such well-meant undulations, usually done with slavish regularity, can easily detract from the broader outlines. Or rather, they can anesthetize the senses to those outlines. If, in addition, they are done with undue rubato, especially on the side of hurrying the pulse rate, the effect is sure to be tasteless sentimentality (or too much "schmalz," to use the musician's piquant term). In any case, interpretation has larger goals. As already implied, expressive details are most valid when they bear out the emotional import of the whole composition and when they point up the form by drawing attention to its focal points, as to a cadence, a new idea, a climax, or a breathing spot. Not seldom, the simplest dynamic plan achieves the greatest breadth and effect. Thus, in Baroque music for harpsichord or organ, in which the dynamic possibilities are limited largely to abrupt contrasts of registers and manuals anyway, it is often most effective to set off the large sections of the form with but one contrasting sign per section—perhaps only an f or p—producing what the Germans call "terrace dynamics."

Where more detailed interpretation within broad sections is concerned, the chief problem is the shaping of phrases. Phrases, like sentences, are so variable in their make-up that one would suppose no generalizations about their performance would hold. Yet, from French theorists, who have contributed importantly to the understanding of expression and rhythm (see Lussy in the Source References), come certain guides to intelligent phrasing— guides of great value to the performer. These guides are especially helpful to the student whose imagination is not yet trained to see the possibilities and whose primary concern is music in the more established styles and forms.

By its very definition, a phrase implies a rise and fall—that is, a beginning, a climactic point, and an ending. Just as a sentence may have one or more subordinate clauses, so a phrase may have one or more lesser climaxes. However, the first problem of the student is to determine the main climactic point toward and away from which the whole phrase should move. The rise and fall of a melodic line is often given as a clue to the rise and fall of a phrase. A rising and falling line does ordinarily mean increased and decreased intensity when it is taken by a voice, or a wind or string instrument, any one of which is most penetrating and brilliant in its highest ranges. And many times it actually proves to mean the same in piano music, too. But, of course, many times it does not. Brahms, for instance, will often increase the volume as he spins out a rich melody that descends into its lowest tones. For

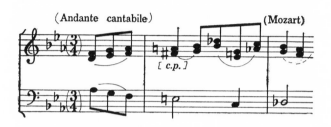

Debussy, "Minstrels," copyright 1909, Durand Edition. Used by permission of the publisher, Elkan-Vogel, Inc., sole representative United States.

EXAMPLE 41

a more comprehensive guide, the following two principles are recommended:

1. In a phrase that contains some unusual feature, that feature becomes the climactic point. The feature may be an unusually expressive harmony, remote foreign tone, sharp dissonance, long tone, high tone, or low tone. Or it may be an unexpected dynamic marking, provided that the marking occurs in a way that permits adequate emphasis (for example, that it lasts long enough). The climactic point in such a phrase may occur even on the first note (disregarding here the contention by some that all phrases begin on an actual or implied upbeat) or on the last note, as in the Debussy illustration in Example 41, which shows three instances of unusual climactic points (marked *c.p.*) in the phrase.

2. Otherwise, the climactic point of the phrase normally occurs on the last "strong" beat *before* the final note. The strong beat, in this sense, is usually the first beat of the measure, though in slow music in even meter it may be the middle of a measure. Example 42 shows two instances of climactic points that are "normally" located (and evidence in the Beethoven illustration that slurs usually mark off smaller units than the phrase).

More often than not the two principles cooperate, confirming

EXAMPLE 42

the location of the climactic point or, rather, leaving no question, especially when the last strong beat coincides with a dissonance yet to resolve (as in the Chopin phrase). Otherwise, questions as to which is the last strong beat, and the like, still leave considerable latitude for interpretation even among the authorities (as in the Beethoven phrase, with A-flat, or the first E-flat, or even the higher B-flat as alternative climactic points). At least, the student now has some basis for his decisions. But there is often a still more basic question to answer—namely, What *is* a phrase? How do you identify musical ideas that vary as widely in length and structure as sentences?

In a good deal of stereotyped music, and in much other music as well, there is the same kind of symmetrical inevitability that one expects to find in a limerick. In such music, the student merely needs to check his phrases off at regular, usually at four-measure, intervals. But in a large part of the serious music he will play, irregular phrase syntax is more the rule than the exception. There are elisions, extensions, overlappings, chain sequences, and truncations without end. Composers like Haydn and Hindemith revel in them. What is the student to do? A detailed answer cannot be given here. But a choice may remain anyway, for after all the irregularities have been classified, one must still return to the definition that a phrase is a musical idea. It is a complete idea, yet it is but a fragment in the larger organization just as it itself is made up of smaller fragments.

Those French theorists say that the primordial atoms in this whole scheme are two- and three-note groups (incises) that overlap a regular or temporary strong beat (ictus) by moving from weak to strong beat or from weak through strong to weak beat. These groups might be found in $\frac{3}{4}$ meter, for instance, as 123|123 or 123|123; and in $\frac{4}{4}$ meter as 1234|1234 or 1234|1234, and so forth. For concrete examples, recall the seven two-note groups and the three three-note groups that make up the phrases, respectively,

"Mine eyes have seen the glory of the coming of the Lord" and "My bonnie lies over the ocean." Even in these short figures there must be rise and fall, because they are, in a sense, embryos of the complete phrase. It is obvious that in the two-note group (termed masculine) the rise must occur on the first note (arsis) and the fall on the second (thesis); and in the three-note group (feminine) the rise must occur on the first note, reaching a peak on the second note, followed by a fall on the third note.

In the sense that energy is required to rise rather than to fall, the first note in each group, although it often occurs on the so-called weak beat, is really a point of lift, or expressive stress. This idea, which may sound to the student like just so much fussy detail, is actually of the greatest importance to intelligent phrasing and to an intelligent sense of musical direction. Yet it is commonly neglected. It applies, for example, to innumerable two- and three-note slurs, which are among the identification tags of the Mozart style (see Example 44 in Chapter 6). Furthermore, it is the basis for the lift that should announce each new phrase and, in a larger sense, for the lift that characterizes the opening A sections of the various two-part (A–B) and three-part (A–B–A) designs.

An allied process can be seen in harmonic and tonal movement. The two-note group may be supported by a chord of suspense on the "weak" beat and a chord of repose on the "strong" beat. In the larger sense of the A–B design, the rise becomes the modulation away from the tonic, and the fall the return to the tonic. In the three-note group, the rise, peak, and fall may be expressed harmonically by *suspension, dissonance,* and *resolution.* In the larger sense of the A–B–A design, it may be expressed by a modulation away from the tonic, the sojourn in one or more new keys, and the return to the tonic.

In the last analysis, any phrase is a composite of two- and/or three-note groups (recall Example 12 in Chapter 2), although forcing conscious attention to these groups might easily have the disadvantage of drawing attention away from the over-all line of many phrases (as in the Beethoven phrase in Example 42 above). Performers must choose constantly between emphasis on the forest or the trees! We have seen that as a composite the phrase itself is like an enlarged two- or three-note group in that it has at least a peak or climactic point and a fall, and more often a rise, peak, and fall. Because such slurs as do mark off phrases in music editing are drawn as rounded curves, one tends to view a phrase as reaching its climactic point normally in the middle. But, as we have also seen, the climactic point is more likely to come near the end (principle 2 on page 144). A more appropriate shape for the slur would be the line described by a streamlined auto fender, with the climactic point at the observer's right.

For the performer, this shape means that the rounding off, or what might be called the low point, of the phrase must take place much more quickly than the (comparatively long) rise to the climactic point. The rounding off gives him concern because, at best, soft playing is more difficult than loud playing. Yet the rounding off is a prime requisite of good phrasing and just as important as the lift at the beginning. It is like sinking into a deep sofa after a hike. To omit it is as frustrating and shocking as to have the sofa collapse. Indeed, abrupt thrusts at the ends of phrases are among the most glaring evidences of musical insensitivity. Especially in a slow phrase with a feminine ending, the performer should try to play the final note no louder than the volume to which the previous note has died away.

In determining the shape and extent of each phrase, the student must not be misled by editorial slurs that pertain not to phrases but to legato passages. While the two uses are sometimes synonymous, their confusion represents one of the serious faults in our notation system. The confusion is even worse for other mediums, where slurs indicate breathing, bowing, and syllabification! Various suggestions have been offered for marking off the phrases, especially the nonlegato sort that dare not have a slur over them for fear they will be played legato. None of these suggestions has attained general use. Therefore, the student must consider the slurs with caution and be prepared to do his own marking off of phrases, abetted by the good counsel of his teacher.

Besides an understanding of form and phrasing, interpretation calls for a familiarity with the styles of different composers, different eras, and different moods. This familiarity depends on long experience. It also depends on a knowledge of authenticity in past styles. On questions of authenticity, the pianist does best to consult the musicologist. The musicologist restores the music as nearly as possible or practical to its original state so that we can distinguish the composer's intentions from all the editorial trappings and alterations that have accumulated over the years. Then he reports on the performance practices of different eras so that we can be faithful, within reason, to the composer's implications. I say "within reason" because the further back we go, the harder it is to reproduce the music exactly as it was meant. After all, most of us play the piano, not the harpsichord or clavichord. On the piano we can simulate the idea of the music only as the piano permits. The piano is simply a different instrument with its own advantages and deficiencies. Too faithful a reproduction of the older music, such as one occasionally meets in harpsichord "transcriptions" for piano, with their awkward imitations of couplings, can only be ridiculous.

Ornamentation is one of the problems of performance practice that teachers and students have become most aware of as a problem. It is also among the most vexing and most violated of performance practices. Up to the time of Clementi and Chopin, when composers began to write them out, ornaments were indicated by a large variety of signs, not necessarily standardized, whose interpretation depended on the period, the locale, the composer, and above all, the context of the music. The serious student who delves deep into the music of the Bach period must expect not only to consult the best editors but to engage in a certain amount of research on his own. Then he will be more qualified to do what must be done in the last analysis anyway, and that is to use his own best judgment. The judgment is required to find a tasteful solution within the allowable limits during the style period in question. Note that it is not a matter of finding *the one* solution to *this particular* ornament (as all too many contest judges seem to assume in downgrading students' performances of Bach). One prime reason for using the signs was not to save ink, space, or effort but rather to allow the performer a certain latitude to improvise solutions within those limits.

Tastefully executed, the ornaments add charm, spice, and points of emphasis in the music. The emphasis results both because ornaments often start on foreign, dissonant tones and because ornamentation is a way of calling attention to a tone, especially on an instrument incapable of stress accents, as the harpsichord or organ is. But ornaments generally do more. At best, they become an indispensable, integral part of the melodic line that was taken for granted yet deliberately left to the performer's art by Baroque composers (see J. A. Scheibe's well-known objection in 1737 to the ornaments already written out by Bach himself, in *The Bach Reader* [New York, 1966], p. 238). Some Baroque ornaments, such as those that occur so thick and fast in Couperin's *ordres* for *clavecin* (harpsichord), cannot quite be done properly on the piano because of its heavier action.

A few basic principles of ornamentation that are still widely disregarded may be restated here for the period approximately from Bach to Mozart. Their applications to specific situations vary, however. In our next chapter, representative applications in specific passages from Bach, Mozart, and Chopin are illustrated and discussed (pages 177–180). For further details, the reader may start with good present-day reference sources like *Grove's Dictionary of Music and Musicians* and the *Harvard Dictionary of Music* where he will find illustrated articles on each of the ornaments (and a valuable index and table under that heading in *Grove*); or he may consult more specialized studies like those by

Bodky on Bach and the Badura-Skodas on Mozart, as listed in our Source References; or he may make use of the practical solutions often provided in the most authoritative performing editions, such as those listed in our Basic Library in Chapter 1; or, best of all for his own initiative, he may go to the primary treatises themselves, like those by Couperin, C. P. E. Bach, L. Mozart, and Türk, as listed in the Source References.

1. Trills in the music from Bach to Mozart generally begin on the upper note. Sometimes an approach from the note below the main note is indicated, and occasionally starting on the main note proves preferable. Chiefly, choose whichever note starts on a dissonance, avoids faulty voice-leading (such as parallel fifths), and favors technical fluency. Trills may or may not continue throughout the note over which they are written and may or may not terminate with a suffix, or windup. The longer the note, the longer the trill is likely to continue, sometimes stopping at a dot or tied note if either follows. The suffix is added when it helps to neaten the end of the trill, as it often does. Sometimes these variants are indicated; more often they are left to the performer's discretion. Like most other ornaments, trills generally start on the beat, mark a climactic point followed by a diminuendo, and lead, legato (with a slur), into the next note. A number of signs are used to indicate the trill, often with no distinction intended. In Bach, the wavy or zigzag sign commonly mistaken for an "inverted mordent" means a trill. But the number of waves has no evident meaning in Bach. The inverted mordent is so rare in music of Bach's period (it is used chiefly in the course of descending scale passages) that every use of it must be seriously questioned before it is accepted. The turn should be thought of as a trill that commences from above or below the main note (as the sign may or may not make clear) and concludes with a suffix from below.

2. Appoggiaturas (leaning notes) in the same music mostly begin on the beat and receive part of the value that is assigned to the main note on the beat. Just what part of the value is the chief

problem. It can be all the way from almost nothing (like the value of the modern grace note if played on the beat) to the entire value (when the main note is followed by a dot, rest, or tie, in which case the main note replaces the same dot, rest, or tie). That guide is helpful in many instances, though hardly always. Another is simply to give the appoggiatura its written value. Still another is to give it half the value of the main note (unless the latter is followed by a dot, rest, or tie, as above). Not seldom all three guides or rules of thumb agree and not seldom, alas, they do not.

Good taste in the matter of dynamics also depends on a knowledge of styles. The "terrace" dynamics mentioned earlier hold good primarily for the period of Bach and Handel but still apply often in the period of Mozart and Haydn. (Such dynamics make good training for the student who monotonously plays everything on the same level. In Scarlatti, for example, he might be asked now and then to play everything *either loud or soft,* but not in between.) Yet it would be quite wrong to think of delicate nuance as the exclusive province of the nineteenth-century Romanticists, just as it would be quite wrong to think thus of tasteful rubato (in the sense of an elastic pulse). The Bach or Handel who wrote such intensely subjective arias in their greatest choral works could hardly have been strangers to these essential means of expression. As for good taste, it consists, again, of knowing the bounds and staying within them. The volume that seems necessary to Liszt will seem out of place and overdone for Mozart.

What is more, the very method of achieving volume varies. In allegro passages by Mozart, as in most lively, strongly rhythmic music, volume can be more a matter of the frequency of group accents than the degree of stress. Thus, two groups of four sixteenths each might be played *piano* by using no accents: *pppp pppp, mezzo forte* by using one accent: *fppp pppp, forte* by accenting the first of each group: *fppp fppp,* and *fortissimo* by accenting every other note: *fpfp fpfp.* On the other hand, in stentorian passages by Liszt, as in other dramatic or grandiose music, each note may be accented separately. To a large extent, these differences are rhythmic in origin. Fast music moves along in groups of notes; slow music permits, even requires, each note to get individual emphasis, the grouping being present but less predominant.

Style and taste both touch on virtually everything else in piano playing, too; much more, in fact, than could be covered in any one book. The playing of contrapuntal music, for example, raises fascinating problems of proper emphasis, of clear distinction between lines, of overlapping rhythms and conflicting directions. To "right-handed" pianists, steeped in homophonic waltzes and nocturnes, this type of playing opens wholly new horizons. In both contrapuntal and homophonic music, the force and sense of the harmony is enhanced by intelligent emphasis on the most influential tones at the moment of each chord change. These tones are more readily identified when they are foreign to the key and hence preceded by accidentals (as in the Mozart phrase of Example 41).

The distinction in degrees of staccato and legato needs constant attention. In slow music, the crisp staccato of a quick piece is ordinarily out of place. In quick music, even the ends of slurs are assumed to be staccato. In a Scarlatti run, the velvety legato of a Chopin *fioritura* (florid, ornamental passage) seems inappropriate. The endless variety of nuance required in poetic performance demands a wealth of attacks, expressive delays, *subito piano* (called "Beethoven piano" when it "tops" a crescendo and often done into the ground as a mannerism), and bold accents. At best, these means might be regarded as the artist's speech, like the endless variety of violin tones that Heifetz or Kreisler used to draw upon. At something less than best, they become his shopworn bag of tricks.

The balance of effects in a composition calls for a fine sense of timing as well as the perspective of musical structure already discussed. In slow movements there is ordinarily time for much grander, more sustained climaxes than in quick movements, where the climaxes, however, may be more impassioned and spectacular. In cumulative sections, there must be breathing spaces where the performer can draw back for his Sunday punch—as Beethoven, Brahms, and Wagner knew so well. He must learn to take one step back for each two forward in order to prolong the climax. Romantic music typically builds around the concept of *the one climax,* often achieved by *the one* consummating harmony. This climax typically appears near the end—recall Wagner's *Tristan,* or the Rachmaninov piano concertos, or the Strauss songs—often followed by a brief, quiet coda, thus reproducing the elongated, "auto-fender" curve in a vastly larger sense.

Whether a climax or drop comes soon or later, students tend to reach it *too* soon. Recall the familiar caution that *cresc.* and *decresc.*, or ⤙ and ⤚, mean louder or softer *later on.* Often, too, every climax is made a maximum effort, especially in the over-excitement of a concert. Giving one's all is a bit like losing one's temper. Preserve that final core of restraint. It implies reserve power and feelings that could yet be tapped but must not be, if only to leave the audience wondering and hungry for more.

All these practices require imagination and experience. Together they produce that sensitivity to musical values that makes for good interpretation. Imagination is a problem in itself. Over and over, the teacher meets with the capable student who turns out one "nice" performance after another, with everything in place and all instructions followed to a T. All that his performance lacks is the spark of re-creative involvement that will bring it to life. Sometimes the student can stimulate this himself by reading the music away from the piano, in complete quiet, and momentarily freed of playing notes. Then he may very well discover a swing or a drive that he had missed in the rhythm, for such innocuous performances usually have an arrhythmic foundation.

Sometimes the teacher can stimulate the student's imagination by his own performance or by the use of meaningful adjectives such as sinister, ecstatic, portentous, frisky, serene, doleful. Indeed, colorful adjectives and adverbs have always been a favorite means by which composers describe their intentions, from Frescobaldi to Scriabin and Medtner. Often artist recordings will provide the necessary stimulus, although their continued use as models for performance tends to atrophy rather than to nourish the imagination. Probably the opposite procedure is more constructive, in which the student makes his own recordings in order to get an objective hearing of his artistic shortcomings. In the main, however, the teacher can go only so far, after which the student will have to light his own inspirational fires.

That Last Mile That Means Perfection

One of the most disheartening truths to face in a frank discussion of piano problems is that so many students repeatedly fall just short of satisfactory performance. Like the indomitable Admiral Peary in his first, abortive attempts to reach the North Pole, they get almost within sight of their goal and are compelled to abandon the project. They spend weeks, perhaps months, going through all the stages of fingering, counting, technical drill, interpretative analysis, and even memorizing, only to find, for one reason or another, that they cannot quite make that last mile that means perfection. What keeps them from going all the way?

The problem may be a specific one, concerned with a particular musical shortcoming. If so, with the odds brought more into his favor, the student should soon enjoy the success that ultimately crowned Admiral Peary's efforts. Or the problem may reveal more deep-seated failings—failings that will or will not submit to extensive treatment. Among specific faults, a common one is simply that of attempting too hard a piece. This can be the fault of the student, who is eager to get to the masterworks that he has tried over or heard in concert, or it can be the fault of the teacher, who is also eager to see his student progress and so continually overestimates his abilities—technical, musical, or both.

The student may attempt a piece that is not too hard but too long—too long for his concentration span in performance and too long for thorough attention to all sections either in his practice or at the lesson. He may get the piece off to a careless start and never quite be able to undo the original errors. This problem is especially common when careless or bad fingering is allowed. He may request or be given an inferior piece not worth the trouble it takes to learn and utterly tire of it before he can work it up to performance level. Or he may leap into a modern or early idiom so foreign to the Chopin, Grieg, and Rachmaninov on which he has thrived thus far that he simply cannot adapt himself in the space of one piece.

Among the more deep-seated reasons for not attaining perfection, defective musicianship and unusual physical clumsiness should be mentioned. These are less common than one might suppose, but when they do exist they are very unfortunate. So often they seem to afflict serious, ambitious students, the kind for whom one would wish the best in the world but perhaps the kind whose chief trait is really love of hard discipline. That these students should be the ones is probably because any other kind of student would have been discouraged much earlier in his piano study. Typical are those who cannot memorize because they lack a musical ear, who cannot play fluently because they do not feel the rhythmic swing, who cannot surmount technical difficulties because their muscular responses are unusually stiff and sluggish. Patient return to musical or technical rudiments may very well bring passable results over a period of time, especially since these students do seem to be the ones most eager to give the time.

Another deep-seated reason is chronic bad practice. Chronic bad practice differs from an occasional lapse in that it indicates an underlying inability on the student's part to apply himself regularly. In fact, it ordinarily represents a personality or adjustment problem only too familiar to every understanding teacher. It shows up most commonly in the brilliant student who goes by fits and starts, with occasional flashes of rare talent and long periods of near-hopeless meandering. By contrast, we may compare the more "normal" student, who may be irritatingly slower in his responses, yet, in the end, somehow manages to turn out one "bang-up" performance after another.

To be sure, the teacher should not expect or, rather, ought not presume to be a psychiatrist. However, he knows that the very nature of music is likely to attract sensitive people with their share of the common neuroses and anxieties. He also knows that the highly exacting requirements of performance, in which the utmost concentration is required and only a fraction of an inch separates accuracy from error, are likely to bring these traits to the fore. Therefore, if he is a mature and sympathetic person, he may at least recognize the symptoms and bear them in mind, perhaps even call them to the student's attention if that can be tactfully accomplished without making him feel that he is a "mental case."

The teacher will understand, in any event, that the old complaint, "He has oodles of talent but is simply too lazy to practice!" hardly tells the whole, or even the correct, story. A physically healthy person who seems outstandingly lazy or careless is very often in actuality a person who is blocked from the effort and patient concentration he himself would like to give by some emotional maladjustment. What that maladjustment may be is, of course, out of the province of the student or teacher to judge. But simply bringing out the general nature of the problem as it affects piano playing and merely removing the stigma of the word "lazy" often help the student to bring in better and more consistent results.

The evidences of some sort of maladjustment will be recognized by student and teacher alike. There is the "fair weather" pianist who practices when everything is just right, which means that most of the time he must beg off or miss lessons with a remarkable assortment of excuses. He is the one who promises to have a much better lesson next time and to institute a permanent reform thereafter. Also, he is the one who, in the more advanced types, somehow gets a sprained finger or wrenched shoulder just before he is scheduled to play somewhere. "Accident-prone," the psychiatrists call it.

Then there is the pianist who always wants a different piece or a different teacher. He complains that he did not get off to a good start or defeatedly berates himself for a bad start, hoping to do much better if he is given a new lease on life. And there is the pianist who shows an almost morbid dread of public performance, chiefly because he takes himself much too seriously. These types and many others sometimes go on for years without conspicuous progress, yet without dropping out, because they love music and in their own ways realize that they have unmistakable talent.

Now, for the "average" or "normal" student, a few suggestions may be given for polishing music that is still short of the performance level. If persistent hitches continue to plague the music, the pianist should first of all look for wrong fingering, uncertain counting, excessive fast practice, or a basic fault in technical method. To make as near certain as human beings can that he has uncovered all the potential hitches in performance, he might try the method of shutting his eyes and counting aloud from memory with the metronome set at a slow tempo. Wherever his finger work or the counting falters, he will know that he needs extra practice.

This method is also an excellent means of maintaining conscious memory of the music—that is, of keeping the memorizing from becoming entirely automatic. As we have seen, memorizing that becomes entirely automatic leaves the performer stranded the moment something interrupts the playing sequence. He tells himself that he played the piece perfectly in the privacy of his home and wonders why he gets stuck now, not realizing that the very different circumstances of actual performance nullify the automatic memory by causing him to observe consciously what he is doing. By now it may be months since he has observed the musical details of that piece consciously!

All pieces should be accurately timed in advance to avoid the embarrassment of too skimpy or too lengthy a program. Frequent timing also helps to keep tab on one's progress. After a piece is brought to performance level, it proves almost as hard to keep at that level as it was to learn. Like the boxer before a fight, one can as easily overtrain as undertrain. Until the day of the program, the piece needs to be kept in cold storage, so to speak, halfway between the evils of neglect and overpractice. I usually have recommended that my students play through such pieces once daily, followed only by what practice proves to be needed on that day.

The period of "cold storage" should be a period of technical and artistic maturation. Therein lies a principal reason for maintaining a repertoire, another being that all of our friends are "from Missouri" and insist on being shown just what can be played. Artistic maturation is certainly a better reason for maintaining a repertoire than several far-fetched reasons that have been mentioned to me, such as a fear that one day a conductor will switch concertos on us unwittingly at the last moment (as seems to have happened to almost every pianist who has written memoirs, not to mention the countless occasions on which "I had never seen the score of the music until it was handed to me on the train en route to the concert").

The student should make a special point of playing right through the piece or program he hopes to present, without a stop, under conditions as near to actual performance as can be attained, and once every day for at least two weeks before the planned date. Otherwise he will be dismayed to learn, as amateur choral and orchestral conductors so often are, that those all-important factors of continuity, breathing spaces, and perspective are still missing. The trouble usually is that the music has been picked apart right up to the last minute. In some pieces (such as the Chopin Etudes), only now will he learn that a real problem of muscular endurance exists, calling for changes that minimize motions and save the strength. The playing-through might well be the first thing done each day. A "cold" performance is about as handicapped as a nervous one. To critical ears it becomes a fair measure both of how ready a piece is and what spots will need most practice that day. It can be still more realistic if one imagines the recital atmosphere, complete even to a sample case of nerves and all the motions from walking onto the stage to bowing and walking off again.

Shortly before the day of performance, the student should go through several dress rehearsals (or "dry runs," to use the more workaday term), calling in a few obliging friends at a time. Their criticisms may do a lot to put final touches on the playing. As the music reaches its last stages of polishing, the student will notice that the problem of concentration comes more and more to the fore. Not only does he have to fight completely automatic memory but he also has to conquer the problem merely of keeping his mind on what he is doing, without letup, especially in a full-length suite or sonata. In most pieces or movements, the pianist is rhythmically bound to keep going without a break from the beginning to the end. Unlike the actor, who is much less rigidly bound to tempo and has at least some relaxation during the other actors' lines to be recalling his own, the pianist has only the breathing spaces that his music permits—and he must make the most of those breathing spaces. Daily performances without interruptions for corrections or polishing gradually help him to locate the slight breathing spaces or rest spots, which are as necessary to the intelligibility of the musical design as they are for the playing. Then he can relax where he used to be tense and he can get deeper and deeper into the spirit of the music itself.

The Worst Bogey of Them All—Stage Fright

Finally, we reach the problem of stage fright, which, whether they will confess it or not, is the worst bogey of all for most performers. No cure has been found that wholly eliminates stage fright, but there are certain facts, attitudes, and procedures that can do a great deal toward alleviating it. These may be introduced point by point.

Nearly everybody gets stage fright. Virtually all performers from beginners to top concert artists experience stage fright. It might be called an occupational disease. Late in their celebrated careers both Artur Rubinstein and Vladimir Horowitz acknowledged that they were still getting "butterflies" before every concert. Students who feel that they are exceptional in being bothered by stage fright should take note.

Being realistic about it helps. If the pianist faces the fact that he will undergo a certain amount of fear when he performs, he may actually reduce that fear somewhat. This he may do, paradoxically, by removing the disturbing uncertainty as to whether he will be troubled by stage fright. The Army has recognized the value of that approach by preparing the men going into battle with, "Naturally you'll be afraid. Who wouldn't be?"

Hiding the fear fools nobody. The pianist who tries to avoid the thought beforehand or tries to tell himself that stage fright does not exist is in for a rude awakening. I knew a young pianist who sought to divert her mind from the fear of playing before an audience by reading Shakespeare just before each concert. The result was that she usually walked onto the stage with excellent composure, only to find herself nearly collapsing after the first few minutes at the piano as the reality of the situation forced itself upon her.

Going to the other extreme can also do harm. Of course, there is always the danger that the realist will exaggerate the problem in his eagerness to recognize it. Then, ironically, he will be defeating the very purpose of his realism. He will no doubt appear on the platform with a scared and harassed expression that will immediately be taken up by the audience, for the performer's demeanor is highly contagious. The moral of this observation is to look proud no matter what happens. If one makes a frightful slip, one must behave like the chess player who wears that just-what-I-had-in-mind look when he discovers he has left his queen *en prise*.

Public performance should be seen in perspective. The performer is right in taking his music seriously and giving his very best when he performs. But he must not take himself too seriously. He needs to remember how it feels to be on the audience side. Some of that mysterious public, that expressionless, unknown group, will really appreciate and value what he does well. Others will undoubtedly yawn and keep tugging at their watches, and there may even be a few who have come to backbite over the least flaw. But that is as it is at all concerts. After all, ninety-nine years from now it will not matter too much how the concert went or what the people thought.

Confidence means knowing the music. The performer who is genuinely confident of himself is the one who is genuinely convinced that he has mastered the music. If there are any misgivings in his mind regarding fingering, counting, technique, memory, interpretation, or other essentials, then he has cause for real fear, not just bogey fear. This point can hardly be overemphasized. The performer may not even be willing to admit those misgivings to himself, but wherever there are shaky passages that result from slipshod or insufficient practice and lack of patience with detail, those spots are certain to cause anxiety. Every pianist who has played in public at all knows with what different degrees of confidence he embarks on an old tried-and-true war horse whose success has been assured by many past performances as compared with a new, untested composition. This fact leads to the related one that

Confidence grows with each successful performance of a piece and diminishes with each failure. The main lesson to learn from this principle is that a piece played without reasonable assurance of success, because of inadequate practice or unfavorable circumstances, may be that much harder to play the next time. Another lesson is that one does not conquer stage fright *in general* merely by more public performance. Rather, he conquers it specifically by more successful performances of a particular piece.

Nervousness should be taken into consideration in practicing. As a part of being realistic about stage fright, the student should practice each passage with the thought that his fingers may very well be jittery when they play it. In other words, he should make allowance for nervousness, which is the product of stage fright, by learning the passage just that much better than would be necessary if he were not nervous. Correct uses of the touch mechanisms, athletically graceful solutions to technical problems, and the covering of as many of the coming keys as possible in "position technique" (discussed on pp. 76–78, 104) help to counteract finger nervousness. One should add that some pianists are not at their best unless they do feel a little nervous. Their nervousness is sublimated into increased energy and sensitivity at the time of performance.

Good physical condition is a kind of antitoxin for nervousness. The performer who is free of colds, unusual pains, outside worries, and fatigue is in a much better position to meet stage fright than the one who is not. By sufficient sleep and healthy living he builds up resistance to the fear of playing. Moreover, he puts himself in the proper frame of mind for the intense concentration that performance requires. It is the highly enervating strain of such concentration and not the physical exertion that leads to nervous exhaustion after a concert. Furthermore, healthy living, including outdoor recreation, lends a robust glow and artistic virility to the playing that seem to counteract fear just as hothouse pallor seems to beget it.

Adequate rest just before the performance is especially important. The performer who has not readied himself far enough in advance will find that last-minute cramming is hardly conducive to self-confidence. It wears him out, fails to "take," confuses what he has already done, and in general makes him anxious. Most pianists develop their own preconcert routines, planned so as to allow them some rest. I myself have liked to be "well slept" before the day of a concert. Early in the day, I prefer merely to "walk" through the program, then avoid undue strain in the day's affairs, eat a very light supper, sleep for an hour, and warm up carefully and easily on scales and other drills a half hour before concert time.

The anticipation of attendant details prevents distressing upsets. Perhaps "details" is not quite the right word for the bow tie that loses itself or the E-flat that sticks just before concert time. Such things can terrify a pianist who discovers them just as he is all set to go. Yet the fault is his for not looking after these things ahead of time. Experienced pianists do not trust to chance but plan ahead. They never assume that the piano will have been tuned, or the keys washed, or the programs proofread, or the publicity handled, or the lighting set, or the proper bench provided, or suitable practice time scheduled where the performance is to be given. A checklist of all possible contingencies is a wise precaution.

Proper warming up gets the program off to a reassuring start.
Pianists dread the cold clammy hands that characteristically go
with stage fright. Sometimes, in spite of the most thorough
warm-up drills, the hands remain chilled and unresponsive. I
should like to recommend the use of a few easy calisthenics and
body-stretching exercises just before going on stage. These get
the blood into circulation and warm not only the hands but also
the whole body. Besides, limbering of this sort provides the muscle
tone necessary for athletic technical requirements. A deliberate
reminder to oneself to breathe steadily is also helpful. This steady
breathing may be necessary to counteract a natural tendency to
hold the breath when nervous, which in turn, I am told, unsteadies
the muscles by reducing the oxygen content in the blood.

*Learning from one's failures does not mean giving up in
despair.* Finally, just this word of caution. The performer who
gives a bad recital must not let that experience scare him out of
ever giving another recital. There is no honest performer who will
not confess to at least one bad recital somewhere in his history.
A bad recital can be highly instructive in a graphic way. The
performer must learn, as the bridge player does, that he has to
lose a good many times in a good many ways in order to become
a consistent winner.

6. Nine Steps in Learning
a New Piece

IN THESE last two chapters, the emphasis is on the pianist's problems of learning and teaching—on "methodology," to use the more awesome term. The particular aim of the present chapter is to propose a sample plan for learning a new piece. This plan is best presented this late in the book because it provides good opportunities to bring together the main points made in earlier chapters and to illustrate them in specific practical situations.

How to start a new piece and what to do then are major concerns of every piano student. If he has no route map, as it were, he may get the general direction but is likely to lose time, get discouraged, or even give up in despair. What he needs is a series of stepping-stones that reduce his journey to shorter, more obvious hops, somewhat as described on pages 3 and 4. No wonder *Gradus ad Parnassum* has been chosen as the title for so many instruction books.

The teacher needs a sequence of procedures to follow in teaching the new piece, too. One sure sign of an inexperienced teacher is the lack of just such procedures. This lack is perhaps more familiar when the problem is to correct faulty playing. However, for either type of problem—correcting faulty playing or teaching a new piece—in the manner of a good doctor, the good teacher must be able not only to diagnose the difficulties or needs but also to prescribe the remedies that will take care of them.

The procedures demonstrated here are recommended for any

pianist who has passed the more elementary stages of playing and is ready, say, for his first Bach Invention. They are not generally recommended, nor is any other inductive method, for beginners, who can get off to a much better start, in my opinion, by taking the sight-reading approach described in the final chapter. The illustrations used in this chapter are taken from relatively advanced pieces so as to include a wider range of learning problems.

By way of a route map, an outline of nine steps to be taken in learning the new piece is offered here. This outline actually consists of the main topics developed in the previous chapters (though in a different order). Furthermore, its three main phases become the three subheadings of the present chapter. In the discussions that follow, most attention is paid to the earlier of the nine steps, these being the steps on which a good foundation depends and the ones that call for the most specific illustrations. But in everyday practicing, the three phases may take about equal time, or an average of two to six weeks each, depending not only on the length and difficulty of the piece but on the method of practice (see pages 125–137).

An Outline for Learning a New Piece

Phase I.   Laying the groundwork
    Step 1. Choosing the piece (balanced diet, quality, length, technical level, and edition)
    Step 2. Understanding the piece (first readings and analysis)
    Step 3. Planning the ways and means (markings, touches, and fingering)

Phase II.   Learning the notes
    Step 4. Fixing the habits and coordinations
    Step 5. Counting with the metronome at a slow tempo
    Step 6. Memorizing (patterns and relationships; more counting with the metronome)

Phase III. Playing the music

Step 7. Counting with the metronome up to tempo

Step 8. Polishing in small-section practice (exercises, touches, pedaling, and tone production)

Step 9. Interpreting the piece as a whole (phrasing, markings, climaxes, continuity, and time to mature)

Steps 1 to 3: Laying the Groundwork

Choosing the piece. The student should be invited to suggest his own choice for a new piece. Too often he is simply assigned the piece, with no questions asked. And too often it will be limited to one of those tried-and-true but shopworn successes that fall into a narrow pedagogic rut. With the richest of all music repertoires to choose from, the pianist's horizons can and should be much wider. Naturally, the student who has access to a basic library of piano music and does daily planned sight-reading in it will know best what he wants.

The choice will depend in part on particular needs. I am not thinking so much of meeting specific technical needs—for instance, choosing a piece because it should strengthen the weak fifth finger. As we have seen, that familiar sort of reasoning puts the cart before the horse. One does better to choose a piece for its musical value and then work on the fifth finger if and as it proves inadequate for that piece. But I do mean that the student who hopes to be well rounded in the field has a need to live at least once with each of those main composers listed in our Basic Library (pages 31–36) and to be at home in the styles and forms of each of the four main eras of keyboard music.

THE FOUR MAIN ERAS OF KEYBOARD MUSIC

Baroque Era, about 1580–1750. Byrd, Bull, Gibbons, and Purcell in England; Frescobaldi and Domenico Scarlatti in Italy; Couperin and Rameau in France; and Bach and Handel in Germany. Age of the harpsichord and clavichord, of motivic writing in more or less polyphonic texture, and of certain options in performance (as in the ornaments). Fugues, suites of dances, variations, and freer types such as preludes and programme pieces.

Classic Era, about 1730–1830. Haydn, Mozart, and Beethoven in Vienna; also, lesser pianist-composers like Clementi and Hummel. Rise of the "pianoforte"; age of more phrasewise writing, the Alberti bass, "singing-allegro," and other more homophonic styles. Chiefly sonatas, concertos, duets, variations, rondos, and fantasias.

Romantic Era, about 1790–1910. Schubert, Mendelssohn, Schumann, Chopin, Liszt, Brahms, Grieg, Fauré, MacDowell, and Rachmaninov. The age of the piano, now enlarged and perfected in its action, pedals, frame, and so on; also virtuoso playing, chromatic harmony, homophony, the *um-pah-pah* bass, idiomatic passage-work, and expression ranging from the intimate and poetic to the grandiose and bombastic. Programme, concert, and character pieces; etudes, rhapsodies, fantasy sonatas, concertos, and two-piano works.

Modern Era, about 1890 to the present. Debussy, Ravel, Milhaud, and Messiaen in France; Hindemith in Germany; Schoenberg and Webern in Austria; Bartók and Kodály in Hungary; Scriabin, Prokofiev, and Kabalevsky in Russia; and Ives and Copland in America. Age of experiments in harmony, tonality, and sonority; percussive touches; return to motivic and polyphonic writing; and complex meters. Forms mainly from the past (as in Neo-Classicism). On the threshold of changes that may radically affect the use, even the future, of the piano.

Unless students are invited into the other three eras, they tend to choose little else but Romantic pieces. They need a more balanced diet, even among the pieces under way at any one time. Ever so often, too, they will want an ensemble piece, as urged in our first chapter, or a "concert arrangement," as of a folk song, or an organ chorale prelude transcribed for piano. The many transcriptions that Bach himself made are good enough precedents for the use of transcriptions. There is no justification, therefore, for blackballing transcriptions as a class, as is done by some purists. The real criteria must always be the quality of the original, the skill of the transcribing, and the adaptability to the new idiom.

Of course, the quality of the piece chosen, whether original or arranged, cannot be graded by any fixed standards—not while music is an art. The safest way to know good from bad at the start is simply to grant that the mainstream of keyboard music has been validated by time and taste. The mainstream is what any student should be bred on first anyway, always remembering that it includes many things besides the most hackneyed pieces. Later he will have the judgment to choose from lesser-known works. Fortunately, most of the great masters from Bach to Bartók left easier pieces, too. These might legitimately be called teaching pieces. Otherwise, one cannot help suspecting much of that large quantity of pedagogic material on the music dealers' shelves. Too much of it has been written by successful, well-meaning teachers who forget that unless they have also had bona fide training in composition and a demonstrated talent for it, they ought to stick pretty much to teaching, leaving the composers to do the composing! Such material is not improved either by the glittering, often very enticing covers in which it is now dressed. A nice cover has a psychological advantage if it is not exploited to hide a shoddy interior. But good music will sell itself. It needs no come-ons, apologies, stunts, or other special inducements.

Other factors in the choice of a new piece are its length and its difficulty (athletic or otherwise) and the matter of a good edition. These were considered on pages 154–155, 90–91, 29–30, 31.

Understanding the music. The learning of a new piece becomes much more effective when the pianist tries first to understand its meaning and form. A survey of musical form is beyond the limits of this book (reference is made again to *Understanding Music* in the Source References), but at least a method of approach can be illustrated here. As in all steps of the learning, the student must do the work himself as far as possible (see pages 94–96).

Bach's fugues pose as much of a learning and teaching challenge as anything in the standard literature. Harder to explain than to hear, they run on in a continuous braidlike texture that must be unraveled to be analyzed, and they cannot be divided into clearly contrasted sections as can the A–B–A and like forms of Classic and Romantic pieces. Bach's Inventions and suite movements pose similar, if less concentrated, challenges. Therefore, for our main illustrations one complete fugue is copied in Example 43 from the *Urtext* of *The Well-Tempered Clavier,* Book I, as published in the Bach-Gesellschaft edition.

Would that every editor and publisher might insert measure numbers, as in Example 43. These are a real convenience not only in this sort of analysis but at the lesson or in a contest, where the teacher or judge can refer to them in remarks jotted down rapidly during a performance. They also permit the teacher to sit at another piano and make references from his own score without getting up each time to point out the measure. When the numbers must be written in, as is usually the case, a good way is to indicate just the first measure in each brace with a heavy figure encircled at the left (as in Example 44). Upbeat measures at the start are not included, nor is an optional ending or a part of a measure after a repeat bar. Separate movements are numbered separately.

To start off, assuming the student reads reasonably well, let him read right through the new piece a few times, coming as close to its musical spirit and style as he can. The purpose is to get some idea of it as a whole and of what the work on it will entail, without playing it enough times for any faults to take root. Following the score a time or two while a good recording is played is a help, too, if one bears in mind the danger of getting overly dependent on the recording (page 154).

To begin the analysis and to be able, later, to keep track of the separate lines or "voices," play each line alone from start to finish.

EXAMPLE 43

Better still, sing and conduct each line in any convenient range, using letter names (see page 10). It helps to label each line according to its range (S, A, T, or B), as is done in Example 43 at the first entries and after each prolonged rest. Dotted lines help to keep track when a line transfers to the other staff, as in measure 10. These shifts and the confusion of upstem and downstem notes on two staffs make the lines harder to disentangle in fugues of more voices (for instance, at measures 85 to 87 of the C-sharp minor Fugue in the same collection).

While the lines are being read separately, the main ideas should be identified so that they can eventually be made to stand out in the texture if and as desired. Each entry of the subject can be marked by some symbol, usually a pair of diagonal lines, as at the fourteen entries marked in our Fugue in F. Any standard contrapuntal devices can be observed at this time, such as the strettos at the octave in measures 36 to 44 and 46 to 54. The example we have taken has no augmentations or diminutions but does include "false entries" (as in the tenor at measures 7 to 9), a decorated entry in the soprano (measures 64 to 68), and hints of inversion (as in the bass of measures 55 to 56), none of which is likely to be mere happenstance in Bach. Any other recurring ideas can now be observed, too, like the countersubject (C.S.) stated by the tenor in measures 4 to 8. The characteristic pedal point in measures 36 to 40 is still another device that needs to be kept in view in performance. As can be seen, what to do with one's spare time is one of the few problems the performer of Bach does not have.

Next, the main cadences in the course of the fugue should be labeled according to key, as at measures 45 to 46 and 55 to 56. Most Bach fugues average two to five internal cadences on any or all of the nearest related keys. These are the main landmarks of fugal form, often defining the goal of a modulatory episode and the re-entry of the subject in the new key. As such, they make the best points for a shift in terrace dynamics (page 142) and for tasteful ritards in the flow, followed by an *a tempo* (as suggested in Example 43). Often they also make the best dividing points (though not in this instance) of the sections by which the fugue can be memorized (page 136).

How does one spot these main cadences? For one thing, in Bach's music the new key is seldom if ever more than one degree away in the circle of fifths. (Can the student name the five nearest related keys to any given key—that is, the five keys whose key signatures differ by not more than one flat or sharp from the signature of the home key?) For another, both the V and I chords are usually in root position. Third, the bass typically repeats on the fifth step (Example 43, measure 55) or makes an octave leap (measure 45) before going to the new tonic. Fourth, the I chord will not be "troubled" by any dissonant tone suspended from the V chord. And last, as noted, the cadence often leads to a re-entry of the subject. Thus, measures 30 to 31 do not qualify as a main cadence, since four of these five clues do not apply.

Planning the ways and means. We have looked over our route map but have yet to decide the exact roads we will be taking. Before the practicing itself can begin in earnest, we need to arrive at the styles, touches, and fingering to be used. Otherwise, as we have seen (page 128–129), we would surely have to retrace many of our steps. Inasmuch as Bach, with almost no markings, poses the main problems again, let him be our point of attack once more.

Always the first problem to be decided is the prevailing tempo, since the choice of tempo must have a profound influence on all else about the music. In fact, in unedited music one often does better not to guess at the character in order to decide the tempo but rather to seek a suitable tempo, which then may well determine the character. There are traditional tempos for many of Bach's fugues. Although today's traditions hardly go straight back to Bach's time, they do deserve some respect for the accumulated musicianship they represent. For our purposes, internal evidence can be a more secure help, even though there is no sure clue to Bach's tempos.

If we were considering Bach's or other Baroque suites, we would get some help from the separate dance titles—allemande, courante, sarabande, gigue, and others—since the speed and character of those dances are known at least in a general way. But in most other Baroque pieces for keyboard, we do not find even the tempo inscriptions—andante, allegro, adagio, and so on—that would lead to one of the five basic tempos described in Chapter 4 (pages 111–113). Therefore, what clues *do* we have? To begin, as in any piece, the tempo extremes can be set by finding the reasonable top speed at which the most difficult or awkward passages can be played and the slowest speed at which the longest note values in the main ideas have meaning. Then, within that range, the tempo is likely to be slower in the fugues that have (1) a thicker texture (in number of voices or closeness of imitations), (2) more changes or diversions in the flow (whether rhythmic, ornamental, or technical), (3) faster harmonic rhythm (more frequent chord changes—recall page 14), and (4) a subject spread over fewer pulses (an interesting but riskier clue).

Finally, there is the long-held idea (dating back to the Renaissance *tactus*) that virtually all music is actually felt at a universal pulse rate close to the heartbeat (and possibly related)—that is, around 60 to 80 on the metronome. This general pulse rate is said to operate not only when the composer specifies it by the time signature or an express marking but when he specifies twice as fast or twice as slow. Thus, Chopin uses the time signature C and the word "Presto" for his Etude in C-sharp minor, Op. 10, No. 4, but in the first edition he approved $\downarrow = 88$ rather than $\downarrow = 176$. Of course, even with a latitude of only 60 to 80, curious questions can arise. In the Fugue in C minor of *The Well-Tempered Clavier,* Book I, how can we prove which is the better of the two extremes, a slower-than-usual speed of $\downarrow = 80$ or a faster-than-usual speed of $\downarrow = 60$? But at least we have this possibility for narrowing the extremes. As to whether a triple grouping is to be heard as one or three pulses, one of the extremes is usually *too* extreme to be considered.

Every one of these clues tends to confirm the general rightness of Bischoff's "Allegretto" and the compound pulse of $\downarrow. = 60$ in

EXAMPLE 44

his edition of Example 43, as the reader can best discover by putting the clues to the test himself. The same clues suggest ♩ (not ♪) = 80 as a suitable tempo for the first movement of Mozart's Sonata in C minor, K. 457, the opening of which is given in Example 44 (after the *Urtext* in *Mozart's Werke*).

Having "captured" an approximate metronome tempo mark in writing, the student should consider next the style of articulation he will want to give to the main ideas and all related material in the fugue. Articulation, sometimes called "the facial expression of music," concerns the slurring and detaching of notes, including the grouping into incises discussed on pages 145–147. Thus, should the subject in Example 43 be one legato line or several groups of slurred and staccato notes? Four possibilities are suggested for measures 1 to 4. Once some such reading is decided, the remainder of the fugue would need to be worked out consistently with this reading (not done in Example 43). Pianists often shy away from taking this sort of initiative and seeing it through to the end. But the arguments are that the music has to be played in some manner, Bach indicated none, and it generally works better to plan that manner than to leave it mostly to intuition and chance. (This last argument raises interesting questions that must be saved for our final chapter.)

To decide the style of articulation presupposes some feeling for historical styles. Baroque music had not yet quite the fussy niceties to be found in Classic music (see page 47). Its style in any one piece was ordinarily simpler and more uniform. Even the details specified by Mozart in Example 44, incomplete (and inconsistent) though they often are, might seem like overloading in Bach. It helps to realize that these styles derived, like violin bowing, from idiomatic techniques. This fact can be seen even more clearly in Domenico Scarlatti's sonatas. Patterns of different note values, as in the subject of our fugue, fall into natural rhythmic and five-finger groupings. Generally, at a moderate tempo, the shorter and longer note values suggest a legato touch while 8th-notes often fall naturally into a staccato or portato touch (recalling the detached cello bowing commonly used for Baroque thoroughbass or "walking bass" in 8th-notes). Usually compatible with that idea is the further guide that stepwise notes are likely to be legato whereas skips are likely to be detached.

Ornamentation and metrically free passages should also be worked out and written down in advance rather than left to chance. These include Baroque and later signs, recitatives, *fioriture,* runs, and short cadenzas. (A student about to study a Classic concerto should get the valuable experience, too, of making up the longer cadenzas himself.) The problem is to work out rhythmic groupings of the notes and any questions of the order, exact pitch, and number of notes indicated by signs. Even free runs are best put into some convincing grouping for fingering, learning, and technical purposes, regardless of whether any rhythmic division is to sound through in performance. Good examples are the free passages in measures 8 and 12 of the Chopin Prelude in F minor, reproduced in full in Example 45 (from the First Critical Edition). But it is not good, even as a teaching device, to fit the notes of a continuous trill into an exact meter, as is so often done in Bach's Two-Part Invention in D minor or Mozart's "easy" Sonata in C major (K. 545) at the long trills. The student who begins by measuring the trill in this fashion has a hard time *un*measuring it later. It is usually best to ease into and out of trills, with the suffix being part of the easing out. Ornaments need to be treated freely and expressively, not rigidly.

Some basic aids for solving ornaments were offered on pages 148–151. But, as suggested there, serious pianists will need to seek more details for themselves. No student can reach pianistic adulthood without a baptism of fire in some richly ornamented piece like Bach's Three-Part Sinfonia in E-flat major in the embellished version or the "Sarabande" from his English Suite No. 3 in G minor. Remember that there is usually not one solution but a choice of solutions within certain limits, the problem being to find

EXAMPLE 45

the best one for a particular context of melody, harmony, rhythm, tempo, mood, and technique.

The ornament signs that happen to occur in our Examples 43 to 45 may be taken merely as samples of questions that are likely to arise. The trills in Example 43 are indicated by a wavy line (which, please recall, does not mean "inverted mordent"!) or *tr.*, without any distinction intended, as is obvious here. The trill in the counter-subject (as in measures 7 or 30) would normally be done the same way each time. To decide exactly *what* way means reaching decisions on the usual three options (page 150). My own preference here (as noted below measure 7) would be to start on the upper note, to trill at once and throughout the dotted quarter-note, and to end with a suffix from below. Even when preceded by the note above, the trill does not necessarily start on the main note; it starts on the main note chiefly when the passage is still quicker or when there is a slur implying that the starting, upper note of the trill is tied to the previous note (as in measure 3 of the "Sarabande" cited above). In measures 7 and 30, starting on the upper note does risk the sound of parallel fifths with the second beat, but the advantage of creating a harmonic dissonance seems to outweigh that risk. The "long" trill in this instance has the advantage of continuing the line to its goal beyond the barline. The suffix is a technical convenience. In measures 45 and 55, the cadential trills are typically short, four-note trills starting on their upper notes and ending at the dots without suffixes. Such trills would be inserted in this dotted cadence formula even were no sign present (as none is in measure 71).

In Mozart the principles are still much the same. The trills in Example 44 start on the upper note (as at the start of K. 576, too). Since Mozart has followed the frequent practice of writing in the suffix, the result is none other than a four-note turn from above, preceded in this instance by the main note as an upbeat. The actual turns in the next movement of this same sonata are all the usual four-note type starting from above, the timing being the chief problem. In the last movement the appoggiatura comes on the beat and follows all three guides given on page 151, subtracting its written value from the next note and receiving half of that next note's value. By Chopin's time the trill was usually started on the main note, as seems best for measure 18 of Example 45, although more often Chopin's own music still sounds better when the old rules are applied.

Not enough is known yet about the widespread practice of "expressive rhythm" in Baroque performance to enable the average pianist to do much about it himself. (See the relevant discussions in Frederick Neumann's book listed in our Source References.) "Over-dotting," or approximate double-dotting, of slower dotted notes is ventured by today's knowledgeable pianists (as in the opening of Bach's Partita No. 2 in C minor). But few dare to apply the sometime eighteenth-century custom of *notes inégales* by giving a quasi-triple, trochaic or iambic, lilt to slower pairs of "equal" 8th-notes. Perhaps our purist attitudes of today compel us to stop short at this license. Or today's pianists may well fear they would be charged with faulty rather than expressive rhythm. The question of whether to match the final, short note of a dotted figure with the final note of a triplet in another "voice," though usually answered in the affirmative in Baroque music, must be considered on a case-by-case basis.

The dynamics signs are still further aspects that must be planned and written in when a Bach *Urtext* edition is used. The nature of the instrument intended could give some historical basis for deciding them. But Bach himself seems not to have wanted to delimit his use of the word "clavier" (to mention the long-time question growing out of the mistranslation "Well-Tempered Clavichord") except in those few instances where he further specified the harpsichord or organ. Even if the harpsichord alone had been intended, one could not play the modern piano and altogether rule out its capabilities for precisely graduated dynamics. Yet, simplicity is the word again. As we have seen, terrace dynamics and broad or brief echo effects were favorite Baroque means of keeping the total structure in view. Based on internal cadences and similar landmarks, a few terrace changes are suggested in Example 43. Note that fugues tend to be cumulative in force but do not always have to build up in volume to the end.

In any new piece, there is one further kind of planning that is best done before the fingering can be worked out and the practicing itself started—that is, the planning for the most efficient touch mechanisms in every situation throughout the piece (see pages 43–49). If these are left to chance with an inexperienced student, the playing can hardly be other than nondescript. For specific illustrations, let us see what situations must be met in our three main examples.

Starting from the beginning of the Bach, the portato dots above the subject and even the staccato dots at this moderate speed indicate notes that are played typically by the full arm worked as a one-piece unit. A break at the wrist would only complicate the control. In measure 2 the full arm, as always, initiates the new slur or handful of notes. It often initiates trills and turns, too, especially when they start by repeating a tone, as in measure 7. The 16th-notes will be played legato by the fingers. After these first few touch situations, no essentially different ones occur in this fairly uniform piece.

The problem is more varied and detailed in Mozart. In Example 44 the heavy staccato tones in measures 1 to 2 and 19 to 22 call for the strength and accuracy of the forearm. The full arm can supplement the fingers to supply a slight accent on the dissonant upper starting note of the trill in measures 2, 15, and the like. This note is the climactic point of the little rise and fall suggested by the added signs and inherent in each feminine incise (see pages 145–147). All slurs, whether in measures 2, 9, 18, 23, or 30, will be initiated, as before, by the full arm acting as the prime mover of the hand to each new coverage of notes. (In measures 16 and 17 the dotted slurs indicate what I take to be Mozart's actual intention.) Hand action best suits the crisp staccato generally understood in Classic allegro music on the last note of a slur not followed by a rest or on independent repeated notes. See measures 3, 27, and 31 for different examples. In measure 3 and similar places the hand has to draw back at the wrist to play the staccato note that ends the slur, then rebound thereafter to repeat this note (as explained on pages 57–58). Forearm oscillation at the radio-ulnar joint can be used to play the broken octaves starting in measure 9, although fingers alone can control them at least as well. In the upper staff of these measures, a finger legato is needed that will be supple enough to permit lateral stretches. The notes in the bass staff from measure 13 are played by the hand rebounding from the wrist until measures 17 and 18, where the full arm best plays such separate, deliberate notes. The tied and slurred chord group that crosses the barline between measures 13 and 14 is really a two-note masculine incise, as suggested by the dotted slur and the diminish sign that are added. To avoid giving a separate impulse to the chord of release (and so making a common fault in technique and musicianship), one must play both chords as though one's arm were passing six o'clock in a steady clockwise arc. The masculine groups across strong beats in measures 30 to 34 and elsewhere can be played in one follow-through motion, too. The best advice for portato repeated notes, as in measure 34, is to stay on the key, keep the same finger, use the full arm from the shoulder with no break at any other joint, and connect the tones as much as possible.

In the Chopin Prelude, Example 45, the full arm again initiates each slur and supplements the fingers to provide any group accents within the runs. The separate 8th-note chords all may be played by the forearms except for the right hand's share during a held note, as in measure 1, where the force will have to come from the upper arm. For better tone control, the last, longer two chords can be started with fingers on the keys and played by the full arms pushing up and forward and permitting a slight give at the wrists. The fast octaves in measures 13 and 14 can be played as a series of diminishing wrist rebounds (or reverberations) initiated by one full-arm impulse. The fast staccatos in measure 18 are best played by strongly articulated finger action (page 55).

The fundamental problem of finding and writing down a good

fingering has been saved for the last topic in this section on laying the groundwork. The reason is that the fingering will be determined in part by the decisions on styles and interpretation. General principles were offered on pages 73 to 80 and 97 to 104. Specific applications are illustrated or cited here. Many of them will appear unconventional, to say the least, to those who have not discovered the values of rapid arm shifts from handful to handful of notes or the freer use of the thumb on black keys. But remember: Anything is fair in love, war, and piano playing!

The fingering should be worked out in detail by taking each hand alone, a section at a time. However, the interrelation of the hands must be watched constantly. If one hand straddles the other, as in measure 6 of Example 43 and in much of Ravel's "Ondine," or crosses the other, as in Scarlatti's familiar Sonata in A major (L. 345, K. 113), then which hand goes over or under and what fingers will be least in the way must be considered. If the two hands are playing parallel passages like those in Example 45, measures 3 to 5, 9 to 13, or 18, then much confusion is saved by making the thumb or other shifts at the same time. Strength and speed in runs can be increased by dividing the run between the hands, which is a possibility suggested in measure 17 of Example 45. However, smoothness would certainly be sacrificed in more delicate passages like that in Beethoven's Sonata in E-flat major, Op. 31, No. 3, first movement, measures 53 to 57 (though the dividing works well in measures 72 to 75). When the hands share notes on the same staff, a thin wavy line can be used to show the distribution that is decided (Example 43, measures 21 to 26).

A good way to begin fingering is to take one handful or coverage of notes at a time, *regardless of what fingers land on which black or white keys.* This modern approach, already mentioned several times, is one basis for today's position technique (page 104) and for the phenomenal virtuosity displayed by some of today's foremost pianists (including some very agile jazz pianists). To find the first handful, simply hold down each successive note until all the fingers are used up. Within the limits of the technique, the starting finger should be the one that permits the largest number of coming notes to be covered while at least one finger serves as a pivot. See Example 44, measures 2 to 3 in the right hand and 3 to 4, or 24, in the left. Two handfuls underlie the choice of fingering in the slurred group of measures 11 to 13. Bridging over rests, slurs, staccatos, or separate arm attacks need make little difference in the application of this principle, nor even small technical disadvantages. See Example 44, measures 17 to 18. The idea is to achieve the maximum simplicity and logic, with the fewest shifts of position (especially shifts by passing the thumb under). Usually simplicity and technical convenience go together. But if there must be a choice, as in a sequence where one of the recurring figures seems to play easier with a different fingering (page 102), then mental ease generally outweighs physical ease as an aid to secure, controlled performance. We have seen that a complicated fingering imperils memorizing. Anxiety in this respect can have a much more paralyzing effect on the technique than an awkward stretch or a taxing use of a weaker finger.

Often it is desirable or necessary to cover more than five notes in the handful or, rather, more than five different pitches, since one may come back to the same pitch several times while covering one handful. If there are six pitches, one finger can do double duty, usually the thumb. If there are seven, two fingers can play twice or the thumb can do triple duty. This extra duty can be managed in several ways. In Example 43, measure 19, the thumb interpolates in a five-finger progression to give a "sixth finger" without disturbing the third-finger pivot on A that lasts into measure 22. In Example 45, measure 10, the slide on both the thumb in the left hand and the fifth finger in the right hand permits six notes to be covered and thus avoids an extra thumb-under shift. In Example 44, measure 23, the second finger actually transfers from G to A-flat in the Alberti bass so that the five tones can be covered by four fingers, saving the fifth finger for the next measure. Working backward from a point at which the fingering is fairly certain was mentioned as a good way to find some of these less obvious possibilities (page 99). In Example 43, by starting back from the third and fifth fingers on which measures 19 to 22 are anchored, the fingering for the handful of seven different pitches in measure 18 can be derived.

Passing the thumb under is done too often, not only within groups of notes better taken in one handful but as if it were the sole means of shifting to a new handful. More resourcefulness is needed, especially in double-notes, to exploit the values of one finger crossing under or over another; of sliding, even from a white to a black key on occasion; or of simply using the same finger twice. Many times in Bach one of these three devices comes to the rescue when the fingering seems to have reached a dead end.

In Example 43, measures 6 to 7, the skip from fifth finger to thumb makes a simple and strong approach to the repeated C that starts the trill. Meanwhile the right-hand fifth finger can play twice, assuming the slurs are used as suggested. In measures 46 to 47, by passing the second finger over the fifth, one shift of position is avoided. In measure 11 the alternative fingerings give a choice of crossing under or sliding. Sliding is convenient in measure 52. The unconventional fingering in measures 54 and 55 stems from the pivot of the third finger on B-flat and requires that the thumb pass *over* the fourth finger to the black key, a very effective technique once its strangeness is conquered. Similar is the crossing over of the third finger in Example 44, measure 2. In Example 43, measures 30 to 33, the handfuls can be preserved and much fuss avoided by simply transferring the thumb and second finger as marked. The legato will suffer no more this way than it does in the more complex solutions usually given. At higher speeds the transfer would hardly be heard (except as clean articulation), any more than the single frames of a movie film are distinguished separately. An odd but successful instance is the use of the third finger on both A-flat and C in the main theme of the finale in Beethoven's Sonata "Appassionata," measure 20.

As pointed out earlier (pp. 59–60), the fourth finger is generally used, and sometimes the third, on black octaves. But these fingers are an advantage on white octaves only when the stretch permits. Sample uses that give a sense of coverage are suggested in Example 45, measure 16. The problem arises often, for example, in the left-hand bass of the main theme in Brahms's *Rhapsody* in E-flat major, Op. 119, No. 4, or in Chopin's "Butterfly" Etude, where a large right hand can start to good advantage with the third finger on top, then use 4–5–4–5–4, and then the same pattern three notes lower. Legato chord connections, as in measures 13 to 14 of Example 44, must be based on total coverage too, with any repeating finger(s) lifted in advance (the thumb in this instance), as explained on page 56. Connecting the top notes is most important, of course. Changing fingers on a repeated note is disadvantageous to control except in two circumstances. Speed may compel the change, as with the 4 to 3 on the two Fs over the barline between measures 14 and 15 of Example 44. And the repeated note itself provides an ideal pivot on which to change hand positions, as in measure 1 of Example 45. Conversely, in measure 13, by repeating the second finger in the right hand, one has the advantage of securing the leap to the chord. In most editions of Beethoven's Sonata in E-flat major, Op. 31, No. 3, a change of fingers is prescribed for the repeated notes in the galloping finale, beginning at measure 12. This change is more than wasteful, since the repeated notes occur in different slurs played by separate attacks of the full arm.

In the innumerable sequences or other recurring figures throughout piano literature, both technical and mental advantages were claimed when each recurrence could be fingered as one handful, with one and the same fingering pattern. See Example 44, measures 21 to 22, right hand and Example 43, measures 68 to 69, both hands. The advantages are made still greater by the recurrence of the figure at the same place in the measure, as usually happens. A longer example is the rotary figure after the middle of Rachmaninov's "Humoresque" (which can be fingered 1–5–4–2 in *every* instance). Such a figure can be set in motion each time by some appropriate thrust of the full arm from the shoulder. When the pianist is enterprising enough to find and get used to these patterns, the results are strength for group accents as desired and that peace of mind gained by not having to watch for a change in some one of the patterns. Ordinarily, one thinks of starting the pattern with an outer finger (thumb or fifth) so that the hand can receive the arm impulse better by rolling with it slightly to either side. Yet the pulsating figure that descends at the start of Chopin's "Revolutionary" Etude is usually and strongly played with arm drops on the second finger to accent the beat (recall Example 11).

Steps 4 to 6: Learning the Notes

The next three steps, in this second phase of learning, need only to be summarized briefly here, since there is but little way to illustrate them beyond the discussions in previous chapters and short of actual practice.

Fixing the habits and coordinations. If there is ever a time when slow, cautious practice is needed or when the motto "Hesitate rather than err" applies, it is when the new habits are getting started. Then a few right playings are more than repaid by rapid progress, and a few wrong ones by slow progress plus the work that must be undone before it can be redone. This need to avoid practicing and learning one's mistakes was emphasized on pages 125 to 128 and elsewhere. So was the need to go right through the piece at this stage as many times as the schedule permits, not stopping to go back or do small-section practice; and the need to practice all aspects of the playing from the start and at once, so that they grow together, including the correct touches.

The exception to this last need is pedaling, which must not be added until the legato, tone balance, and other touch habits can be formed and observed critically, much as violin vibrato is best delayed until the bowing and intonation are worked out. If necessary, the counting aloud may be prepared by clapping the more intricate rhythms in advance (pages 108–109), and each hand may be played alone at first to reduce the number of things to keep in mind. Then, when the hands are first combined, special care must be taken. For them to coordinate the various conflicting lines, rhythms, or touches such as occur in Examples 43 and 44 presents a pat-your-head-and-rub-your-tummy problem. Besides, a particular touch that proves to be the only possibility at a fast speed may seem awkward at the slow practice tempo—for instance, the use of the wrist to play the octaves in Example 45, measures 13 and 14. It is too bad such places cannot be played fast from the start. But they cannot, and they must be practiced as they will be played. If the student cannot manage to look before he leaps into mistakes, he might try stopping *before each note* to ask these questions: What is the note? Is it changed by an accidental? Which hand and finger play it? What count, if any, does it fall on? In what style is it played? What touch mechanism is used? This method may seem far removed from the musical goal, but it is hard to be musical until the right notes can be assured.

Counting with the metronome at a slow tempo. (See pages 105–106.) This work with the metronome is the first of the steps that will take the piece off one level and boost it up to the next. Even at a slow tempo, the notes that were but isolated sounds before will now begin to be heard in larger musical relationships, whether of melody, rhythm, harmony, or the total structure. The new step should begin as soon as the conscious note reading (if not peering) ends and the habits have clearly become habits, strong enough to withstand an error now and then. If even the slow tempo seems too fast, the beat may be subdivided at first so that the metronome comes on the "ands" as well.

Memorizing. Memorizing slows the piece down at first but soon proves to give it another big boost. On pages 131–137, the types and general methods of memorizing were discussed. Do not forget to keep the score out of sight while playing, from now on. Much will have been memorized already, at least partly, thanks to patterns and relationships made apparent during analysis of the music and during fingering. Among further patterns and relationships to look for, sequences are outstanding aids, especially when the figure, meter, and fingering tally, as discussed earlier. When the entire piece can be recalled, however haltingly, the most effective way to clinch the memory is to start counting from memory at a slow tempo with the metronome again.

Steps 7 to 9: Playing the Music

Counting with the metronome up to tempo. Here is still another boost for the piece. It applies chiefly to pieces that are fast or otherwise difficult for the learner. The effort to play up to tempo may mean some splashing and struggling along the way. But there may be no other way to achieve the higher speeds, and the correct habits should now be beyond easy corruption. Often, playing successive handfuls as simultaneous clusters helps to pull up the tempo (pp. 76–78). For the most efficient touches, without waste motion, and for the ease and security that come with reserve power, the metronome may be set, on occasion, five to ten per cent higher than needed. But slow practice must be reintroduced at regular intervals in the practice, too, if the habits are not to start breaking down. (See pages 129–130.)

Polishing in small-section practice. The efforts to bring the piece up to tempo will bring to the fore those hardest spots that did not fall into line during any of the earlier steps. Now is the best time to conquer them, practicing in small sections where necessary. The method recommended more than once here is to create exercises out of these actual situations. Besides the procedures mentioned on pages 89–93, a method of converting figures or handfuls into double-note exercises may now be described. This last procedure quickly reveals the weakness in a figure, or in one's technique, for that matter, since it gets at the real criterion, which is finger independence and coordination, not mere noise and uncontrolled speed. It usually corrects the weakness, too, by developing both the feel and best angle of the hand for the cluster and the weak coordination in question.

The double-notes are found by taking each possible combination of notes within a figure of three, four, or five *different pitches* (which may mean many more notes). In effect, one permutes the figure. Thus, in Example 43, if the three pitches used in the trill and suffix in measures 7 to 8 do not play smoothly, the bottom two can be played as one double-note and alternated with the top one tremolo fashion, or the top two with the bottom one, or the outer two with the inner one. These pairings can be represented by the suggested fingering: $\frac{2}{3}$ vs. 1, $\frac{1}{2}$ vs. 3, and $\frac{1}{3}$ vs. 2. In all exercises of this sort, a legato yet exaggerated finger action must be used, with no arm jogging (pages 50–51), and the alternation must be in triplets so that each member of the pair gets its share in the strengthening benefits of the accent. Timesavers and devotees of limbering exercises might well let the other hand come along for the ride, too. The four-pitch group in the trill from measures 2 to 3 in Example 44 can be practiced: $\frac{3}{2}$ vs. $\frac{5}{4}$, $\frac{4}{2}$ vs. $\frac{5}{3}$, and $\frac{5}{2}$ vs. $\frac{4}{3}$. And in Example 45, measure 11, the five-pitch group on the last beat can be practiced (to take just the right hand): $\underset{1}{\overset{3}{2}}$ vs. $\overset{5}{4}$, $\underset{1}{\overset{4}{2}}$ vs. $\overset{5}{3}$, $\underset{1}{\overset{5}{2}}$ vs. $\overset{4}{3}$, $\underset{1}{\overset{4}{3}}$ vs. $\overset{5}{2}$, $\underset{1}{\overset{3}{3}}$ vs. $\overset{4}{2}$, $\underset{1}{\overset{5}{4}}$ vs. $\overset{3}{2}$, $\underset{2}{\overset{3}{1}}$ vs. $\overset{5}{1}$, $\underset{2}{\overset{4}{1}}$ vs. $\overset{5}{1}$, and $\overset{4}{3}$ vs. $\overset{2}{1}$! But if this much detail almost kills the patient in order to effect the cure, he can try the simpler combination of five pitches: $\underset{1\ \ 2\ \ 3\ \ 2}{3\text{–}4\text{–}5\text{–}4}$ and so on, always remembering the value of the triplet rhythm.

If no such remedy helps, perhaps a different fingering, distribution between the hands, or touch mechanism can be tried. Or perhaps the passage is a climactic one where the pianist can make a virtue out of his difficulties by broadening the tempo a bit (as at the final canon and subject entry in Franck's *Prelude, Choral, and Fugue*). Or, assuming the rest of the piece goes well enough, it may even be necessary to thin out or simplify the notes themselves a bit on the theory that the total effect is more important than the details. This last secret of the trade is a musical sacrilege, to be sure, but one that seems to be the rule rather than the exception in some pieces (for example, the opening of Ravel's "Ondine").

Other polishing is in order at this point, too. The touches must be re-examined to see if they are affording the most economical and athletically graceful solution to each situation—the best follow-through, swing, elasticity, "dog-paddle" alternation of the hands, or other coordination *as these may help to further the music's meaning*. The joints must not break unnecessarily. (Recall the rubber-handled hoe.) Is the staccato crisp enough for its context? Is the legato faulty because of failure to hold the arm still, stay on the keys, cover the handfuls, stretch laterally, pedal clearly, or group the tones sufficiently?

The pedaling itself needs special attention now. (See pages 121–125.) Polyphony at most permits only careful "flutter" pedaling except where there are chords to enrich, as at cadences. A melodic line must be heard as a line. Even when it outlines chords, as does the subject of Bach's Two-Part Invention in A minor, it must not be reduced to a diffuse chordal mass by the pedal. Thus, in Chopin's Prelude in D-flat major the pedal is best delayed at the start until at least the second if not the third melody note is reached, the more so in a descending chord outline because the highest tone would continue to predominate. Pedaling through rests is often questionable. For example, notwithstanding contradictory pedal markings, Chopin seems to have meant what he wrote in the Scherzo in B-flat minor, measure 5, when he put a staccato under the B-flat and two quarter-rests after it. This effect, of a startled gasp before the crash, can be very dramatic.

While listening critically to the pedaling, the student must *hear* the melody tone and the total sonority he is producing (pages 118–119). Is the balance good, with not too much bass, with enough melody to "sing," yet with no tones missing in the harmony? Does each melody tone get about equal emphasis, with no loss of importance because it is on a weak beat, or short in duration, or the bottom of a leap? Whatever the touch, it is always harder to play soft than loud. Getting closer to the keys and lowering the wrists often help, as, for example, in a delicate piece like Mendelssohn's Scherzo in E minor.

Interpreting the piece as a whole. This final step is needed in order to see more clearly the forest of which the trees are a part (page 141). Every aspect of interpretation must be reconsidered to see whether it is contributing to the final goal, which might be stated as meaningful projection of the total form—or more simply, as getting the musical message across.

The markings need to be rechecked at this time. Original markings are a free lesson from the composer and certainly the most authoritative lesson of all. How often a student will work hard on a Debussy Prelude without ever thinking to look up the meaning of the instructions very precisely worded in French! The prescribed dynamic and tempo levels must be heeded especially, so that the valleys and peaks of the form are in good perspective, from the most relaxed moment to the over-all climax (page 142). The same perspective must be sought even throughout the contrasting movements of an extended suite or sonata. The pianist who tries to maintain the pressure and excitement all the way, with no letups, only defeats his own purpose. Mature artists do not anesthetize their audiences in this way. By giving meaning to everything, they can afford to play much of the time in a quiet "speaking voice" and well under their top speed, making the few real climaxes far more exciting.

Every phrase needs to be re-examined to see if its meaning is clearly understood. Does it go to and from somewhere? Is there a climactic point that is musically convincing (pages 142–145)? A useful rule of thumb is the one that says no note should occur twice in the same phrase in the same way.

Occasional rechecks with the metronome keep the prevailing tempo in mind and ward off eccentricities in the performance. Driving music must keep driving; all the while the train is passing all sorts of scenery or going through tunnels, the tackety-tack of the railroad ties keeps up its steady beat. On the other hand, there must be those breathing spots that can come only after many playings. These occur, of course, at phrase endings, and more so at the broader and broader divisions in the form. They are sometimes equally necessary for endurance (page 159).

To bring all these factors together in one unified, convincing, well-controlled performance takes many complete playings of the piece and a fair amount of time. One must figure on several weeks or more between the day when the piece has first been played up to tempo without hitches from memory to the day of the first public performance. During that time the piece should mature and change from a "new piece" to a piece in the pianist's repertoire.

7. *Il Maestro e lo Scolare*

THIS BRIEF concluding chapter borrows its title from that charming duet by Haydn in which each variation by the teacher is faithfully imitated by the pupil. It deals, in fact, with two interesting questions of teaching methods that have been at the center of numerous books, articles, and discussions in the piano world of recent years. One concerns a new approach to piano study through sight-reading, the other a comparison of learning by facts with learning by intuition and imagery. My own inclinations in these matters are made clear enough in this book. But it should become equally clear that no single, final answers are either necessary or possible. Too much depends on the individual background, personality, and educational philosophy of each teacher and on the background, propensities, and talent of each student.

An Approach Through Sight-Reading

In a significant little book called *Guided Sight-Reading,* the late Leonhard Deutsch explained his method of developing pianists from scratch to advanced performers entirely through sight-reading. For the details and some real nuggets of teaching wisdom, the reader is urged to see this book for himself (listed in Source References). Here the remarks deal only with the use of the method in the first year or so of study and with what some of us have concluded through our own experiments to be in many ways a more sensible approach than the traditional, inductive one.

Traditionally the beginner is introduced to piano playing one item at a time in a logical sequence. "This is a piano. You sit in front of it, so. There are eighty-eight white and black keys. See how the black keys are arranged in twos and threes. Middle C is to the left of the two-black-key group and in front of your nose. Play middle C with this thumb." And so forth! Not so with Mr. Deutsch. In effect, he seats the beginner at the piano, with the first little piece on the rack, puts his finger on the starting note, and tells him, "O.K., begin playing. When the notes go up, you go up; when they go down, you go down." The "guided" part of the sight-reading means mainly that the teacher plays along with the student in a higher octave or at a second piano, thus giving him the idea of the music and the support to keep it going. Explanations are given *only as the student needs them* to advance in this manner, or *as he himself requests them.*

Mr. Deutsch's argument, paraphrased and slightly expanded here, is that the beginner does not learn inductively, step by step, but reaches at once to reproduce the total result as best he can. A child learns to walk not from gradual training in the use of the fibula and metatarsus, or some such, but by imitating grownups as he struggles right off to get to the cookie held before him. The refinements come later.

Six important advantages might be claimed for the sight-reading approach, which goes even further and more directly into piano learning than rote teaching or the various five-finger position systems. First, the immediate, ever-present incentive or goal is music itself. *One learns piano to make enjoyable music.* This is a goal easily lost sight of at any stage of learning, what with so much emphasis on the means to the end—on trick methods, exercises for their own sake, pretty covers, or other inducements mentioned in the previous chapter. Second, *the student experiences success at once.* Neat explanations that seem so necessary and systematic to the initiated simply try the patience of the novice. In fact, they can soon kill his interest because they seem so remote from the goal.

Third, *all practice is supervised at first,* that practice being the lesson itself (a recommendation that only the parents may not readily understand and accept). When the beginner is a young child, to expect straight, independent practice often seems unreasonable. An ideal schedule, even for the supervised practice, might be one that permits each child to come for, say, three ten-minute lessons a week rather than one half hour. Fourth, the sight-reading approach *permits the learner to discover meanings and relationships for himself.* When he does discover them, they are likely to make more sense than the most logical, careful explanations from an outside source. It is strange what curious gaps those "logical" explanations often leave in the student's mind.

Fifth, this approach *favors reading not by single pitches and note values but by contours, groups, and patterns* (in the manner that children are now taught to read words, in spite of recent controversies). The approach may be hard for some to accept, but the line and staff and the note values are learned much more readily in this way and with the details only filled in as the student requests them (if he has not discovered them for himself!). Sixth and last, the teacher who turns to this newer approach is likely to feel that he himself has won *a new lease on his teaching life.* Gone is the struggle to win and hold the interest. The music itself wins the student over and keeps him.

The object in these first years is not perfection but broad keyboard experience in as varied and as much music as possible. (Deutsch himself left a collection of charming folk-song arrangements for this purpose.) It seems strained and optimistic to insist on refinements, such as any special hand position, at a time when gross motor controls are still being learned. The child totters precariously before he himself corrects his form. Public recitals may well be only a barrier in early training (another recommendation that the parents in particular may not readily accept). Technique work could be limited to simple exercises that develop a feel for the spacing and geography of the keys and an awareness of the four playing mechanisms (see pages 43–49). For the fingers, the chromatic scale in the standard fingering and the sequential pattern of the first of the Hanon *Daily Exercises* can be learned with surprising ease. For the hand, parallel thirds played by the second and fourth fingers of both hands up and down the white keys answer well. The forearm can do triads fingered 1–3–5 in the same manner, while for the full arm the beginner enjoys inventing his own hand-over-hand patterns that repeat at each octave level, "dog-paddle" style. Going from the bottom to the top of the keyboard and back is a good way to define the extent of these exercises. (The littlest tots cannot sit but have to walk to do this.)

My own belief is that Mr. Deutsch's approach is excellent at the beginning (and always as a means of developing sight-reading itself) but it must presently be replaced by something like the inductive one detailed in the previous chapter. In other words, as the student gets more and more into single works that he would actually like to perfect and perform he must change more and more to systematic, step-by-step learning. Prior to that stage, in the realm of elementary training, enterprising and adventuresome teachers may find that the sight-reading approach can revolutionize the traditional teaching methods.

Learning by Intuition, Imagery, or Facts?

In recent years, not only Mr. Deutsch but Luigi Bonpensiere, Abby Whiteside, Lilias Mackinnon, and others have written highly stimulating books that argue largely for a more direct approach to the whole musical composition, or *Gestalt,* as the sum of more than its parts. Rightly or wrongly, they have come a long way from the stern factual discipline that infuses the treatises in which the great masters of the past somehow found what they needed and wanted. Whether the new approach is through rhythm, mental attitude, or other means, the idea is to avoid getting sidetracked by minutiae and abstract intellectualisms. Objections are voiced against what one author aptly calls "notewise" practice and the self-conscious, studied performances it might produce, and against systematic explanations about what is essentially an art and not a science. Similar to Mr. Shepherd's thoughtful remarks quoted on pages 115 to 116, the remarks by these authors suggest that concentration on an aural image of the piece will direct the learning subconsciously, more efficiently and musically than any conscious, piecemeal methods of building up to performance level.

These authors themselves have all done successful teaching. Furthermore, one cannot deny, on the one hand, that their first interest is a thoroughly musical performance and that psychological aids can be very effective (see pages 153–154) or, on the other, that academicians can easily miss that extra something that fulfills the *Gestalt*. For my own part, I think of only three reservations to be made—cautions rather than objections—in the interest of less experienced teachers.

First, the momentum of even the fastest running start toward the goal cannot pick up *all* the details along the way. Certain ornaments simply will not solve themselves, certain fingering will not see ahead to what must come out, certain touches will not co-ordinate without very considerable stopping for analysis, planning,

and that notewise practice. Second, there is always the danger that the psychological inducements (the "python-like writhings," "drum-beat," or "beckoning with a handkerchief" that Bülow and Lebert asked for in Beethoven) will be exaggerated to the point of causing actual errors of fact and method. Familiar examples are the strange touches sometimes developed to evoke differences of timbre (at the same volume) that simply do not exist (although more remarkable examples could be cited from vocal instruction!). Third, it is sometimes easier and clearer just to state the facts. As Arnold Schultz wrote about tone (*The Riddle of the Pianist's Finger,* page 196),

> My own objection to the theory of voluntary control over tone-quality is based less upon the relationship of the moving hammer to the strings and upon photography of sound waves (although this evidence seems incontrovertible enough) than it is upon the fact that what people designate as qualitative differences are explicable in simpler and more satisfactory terms.

But there really ought be no great divide between the extremes of subjective and objective teaching. The ideal teacher to break through this divide, I should think, would be the one capable of fitting the approach to the student. And he would be the one with the imagination to stimulate the larger view, yet with the solid grounding by which to avoid leading his students astray into more or new pianist's problems.

SOME SOURCE REFERENCES FOR ENTERPRISING PIANISTS

Some students and teachers will want to peer behind the scenes into the evidence for what they have read here. Others will want further details about musical form, the history of the piano, performance practices, phrasing and articulation, technique, and other related subjects. Here is a list of representative publications that should prove helpful. It is but a sampling, of course, among many more such books that might well have been included (see Maurice Hinson's two bibliographies listed below). Reviews are cited when they supply expanded previews of the books listed.

American Music Teacher. A periodical issued six times yearly by the Music Teachers National Association, 1831 Carew Tower, Cincinnati, Ohio 45202. Regularly includes articles of special interest to piano teachers and students as well as some reviews of new piano teaching materials.

Apel, Willi, *Masters of the Keyboard: A Brief Survey of Pianoforte Music.* Cambridge Mass.: Harvard University Press, 1947. In spite of gaps and some errors, still valuable for its authoritative views and for many complete music examples from about 1500 to the twentieth century. Reviewed in *Notes* (Journal of the Music Library Association) for December 1947.

Bach, Carl Philipp Emanuel, *Essay on the True Art of Playing Keyboard Instruments* (1753–1762), translated by William J. Mitchell. New York: W. W. Norton, 1949. The most celebrated treatise of the eighteenth century, with much information on fingering, ornamentation, and style that bears at least tangentially (a generation later) on his father's music. Many examples. Reviewed in the *Piano Quarterly* No. 14.

Badura-Skoda, Eva and Paul, *Interpreting Mozart on the Keyboard,* translated by Leo Black. New York: St. Martin's Press, 1962. An essential, up-to-date study that often applies to Haydn, early Beethoven, and other Classic composers, too. Many examples. Reviewed in the *Piano Quarterly* No. 43.

Bodky, Erwin, *The Interpretation of Bach's Keyboard Works.* Cambridge, Mass.: Harvard University Press, 1960. The most extended and comprehensive of numerous books on this topic, including valued personal conclusions. Many examples. Reviewed in *Notes* for March 1962.

Butler, Stanley, *Guide to the Best in Contemporary Piano Music: An Annotated List of Graded Solo Piano Music Published Since*

1950. 2 vols. Metuchen, N.J.: The Scarecrow Press, 1973. Covers "levels 1 through 8." Enriched by full, practical comments.

Clavier. A periodical issued six times yearly by the Instrumentalist Co., 1418 Lake Street, Evanston, Ill. 60204. Devoted primarily to piano playing, teaching, and music.

Couperin, François, *L'Art de toucher le clavecin* (The Art of Playing the Harpsichord; 1716–1717). Trilingual edition (French, German, English). Wiesbaden: Breitkopf & Härtel, 1933. A short treatise of the early eighteenth century, important especially for French music. Many examples.

Deutsch, Leonhard, *Guided Sight-Reading: A New Approach to Piano Study.* New York: Crown, 1950. See the discussion in our Chapter 7. Supplemented by two graded volumes: *For Sight Reading—59 Folk Songs of Various Nations* (Heritage Music Publications). Reviewed in *Notes* for March 1951.

Dolge, Alfred, *Pianos and Their Makers,* 1911, paperback reprint. New York: Dover, 1972. Although somewhat outdated, still valuable for its rich illustrations and informative lists.

Donington, Robert, *A Performer's Guide to Baroque Music.* New York: Charles Scribner's Sons, 1974. Explores questions of feeling, style, the instruments (not confined to keyboard), accidentals, ornaments, accompaniments, tempo, rhythmic licenses, and dynamics.

Harding, R. E. M., *The Piano-Forte: Its History to 1851* (1933). Reprint. New York: Da Capo, 1973. The standard account in English; detailed, documented, and fully illustrated.

Hinson, Maurice, *Guide to the Pianist's Repertoire,* edited by Irwin Freundlich. Bloomington, Ind.: Indiana University Press, 1973. Annotated listings by composers, including music publishers, bibliographical references, contents of anthologies, special indexes, and other useful information. (Supersedes *Music for the Piano* by J. Friskin and I. Freundlich.)

Hinson, Maurice, *The Piano Teacher's Source Book: An Annotated Bibliography.* Melville, N.Y.: Belwin-Mills, 1974. Books for the pianist, listed by categories, including accompanying, aesthetics, analysis, biographies, church music, class piano, construction and design, history, lists of piano music, ornamentation, pedagogy, and performance practices; supplemented by special indexes.

Keller, Hermann, *Phrasing and Articulation*, 1955, translated from the German by Leigh Gerdine. New York: W. W. Norton, 1965. Discussions by eras, with three chapters on Bach and one each on Mozart and Beethoven. Many examples. Not a distinguished book, but one of the few in English on the subject. Reviewed in *Journal of Research in Music Education* for the summer of 1966.

Kirby, F. E., *A Short History of Keyboard Music*. Riverside, N.J.: Free Press, 1966. In spite of some errors and evidences of haste, the most comprehensive, knowing book yet available on the subject. Reviewed in *Notes* for March 1967.

Loesser, Arthur, *Men, Women and Pianos: A Social History*. New York: Simon and Schuster, 1954; paperback reprint, 1964. The rich lore of pianos, piano playing, and pianists in social history, foreign and American; highly informative and entertaining.

Lussy, Matthis, *Musical Expression*, translated from the French. London: Novello, Ewer, and Co., 1885 and later editions. A primary study of the shaping and direction of the phrase. Many examples. See our Chapter 5.

Mozart, Leopold, *A Treatise on the Fundamental Principles of Violin Playing* (1756), translated by Editha Knocker, preface by Alfred Einstein. New York: Oxford University Press, 1948. An illuminating, mid-eighteenth-century treatise that relates to Leopold's famous son and often applies as much to keyboard as to violin playing.

Neumann, Frederick, *Ornamentation in Baroque and Post-Baroque Music*. Princeton, N.J.: Princeton University Press, forthcoming. Likely to become the definitive work on the subject. Detailed, richly documented, with many examples.

Newman, William S., *Performance Practices in Beethoven's Piano Sonatas: An Introduction*. New York: W. W. Norton, 1971. Examples and illustrations. Reviewed in *Notes* for June 1972.

————, *Understanding Music: An Introduction to Music's Elements, Styles, and Forms—for Both the Layman and the Practitioner*. 2d rev. ed. New York: Harper & Row, 1961; paperback reprint (with changes), 1967. A background for pianists and others. Reviewed in *Notes* for March 1962.

Ortmann, Otto R., *The Physiological Mechanics of Piano Technique: An Experimental Study of the Nature of Muscular Action as Used in Piano Playing, and of the Effects Thereof on the Piano Key and the Piano Tone* (1929). Paperback reprint. With an introduction by Arnold Schultz. New York: E. P. Dutton, 1962. The most basic and significant study of the subject from a scientific standpoint. Illustrated.

Piano Quarterly. A periodical published quarterly by Belwin-Mills, 25 Deshon Drive, Melville, N.Y. 11746. Superior articles, readers' columns, reviews of music and books, and "thematics" for piano teachers, students, and performers. Copiously illustrated.

Schultz, Arnold, *The Riddle of the Pianist's Finger and Its Relationship to a Touch Scheme* (1936). New York: Carl Fischer, 1949. A keen analysis of the physiology and leverage problems of piano technique, and a critique of the approaches by Leschetizky, Matthay, Breithaupt, and Ortmann. Reviewed in *Piano Quarterly* No. 13.

Seashore, Carl, *Psychology of Music* (1938). New York: Dover, 1967. Concerns learning and the musician's capabilities.

Stevens, Floyd A., *Piano Tuning, Repair, and Rebuilding*. Chicago: Nelson-Hall, 1972. Clear, well illustrated. Includes use of the Strobotuner to set the temperament.

Sumner, William Leslie, *The Pianoforte*, rev. ed. New York: St. Martin's Press, 1966. Includes history, construction, composers, and piano lore. Many illustrations.

Index

74 75 76 77 10 9 8 7 6 5 4 3 2 1